S0-AYC-210

DISCARD

JUSTICE
IN
AMERICA

J. Cheney Mason

PUBLISHING

Copyright © 2014 by J. Cheney Mason

FIRST EDITION

All rights reserved. No part of this book may be reproduced in any form or by any electronic or mechanical means, including information storage and retrieval systems, without permission in writing from the publisher, except by a reviewer who may quote brief passages in a review.

Library of Congress Cataloging-in-Publication Data
Available upon request

For information, or to order additional copies, please contact:

TitleTown Publishing, LLC
P.O. Box 12093 Green Bay, WI 54307-12093
920.737.8051 | titletownpublishing.com

Published in the United States

Distributed by Midpoint Trade Books
www.midpointtrade.com

Printed in the United States of America

Interior design by Vally Sharpe
Cover Design by Jessica Ciesluk-Hunter

Dedication and Acknowledgments

To my wife of 41 years (so far), Shirley, who has supported my career through several hundred trials and untold tribulations. Without her, I could not have survived Casey's trial and all of the insane fallout.

To Casey, who has endured the unthinkable with the courage of a lion, and to whom much of the world owes an apology.

And finally, to twelve of the most courageous citizens who should forever hold their heads high and proudly for doing their job—the jury.

In addition, thanks are due to attorneys Lisabeth Fryer and Dorothy Clay Sims, draftees for the defense team, without whom our success in saving Casey's life would have been near impossible; to my assistant Diana Marku, who had to do much of the labor and all of the screening to make the trial survivable; to my long-term suite-mate, attorney Don Lykkebak, who constantly provided support and stabilized my practice during the long ordeal; to Karen Rhine, the court reporter who took over a hundred depositions for the defense at the "indigency rate" and provided all of the typing for this book; to Ed Bailey, who helped in my drafts with his input as a psychiatrist; to James Carpenter, the final editor who provided invaluable assistance with the final organization and editing; and of course, to Tracy Ertl of Title Town Publishing, who pursued me to write this book and would not take "no" for an answer.

TABLE OF CONTENTS

INTRODUCTION

I should say, to begin with, that this book is about more than my client Casey Anthony and her trial. While it does include much about her case, and reveals the truth behind the accusations against her, as well as behind the legal process and its abuses during her trial, its main concern is in fact a much larger one. Our society—and unfortunately, it would appear, much of the world—has a very distorted understanding of what is, or at least should be, meant by the term "justice."

Justice is a concept of moral rightness based on ethics, rationality, law, natural law, religion or equity. This is a definition attributable originally to Plato; if we look to more modern times, specifically to Webster's Dictionary, we find justice most generally defined as "the quality of being just, impartial or fair"—"the maintenance or administration of what is *just*, especially by the impartial adjustment of conflicting claims or the assignment of merited rewards or punishments."

Nowadays, unfortunately, as a result of lack of understanding, miseducation or simply gravitation toward a spirit of meanness, all too many people equate the term "justice" with the concepts of vengeance or punishment. It may well be that, in many circumstances, arriving at a concept of moral right-ness may include punishment. It does not, however, follow from this that pun-ishment and penalties constitute the central point of the concept of justice.

In this book, we will explore the application of the term "justice" as it pertains to a specific practical problem: namely, to its obstructions during the Casey Anthony murder trial. Yet the problem is by no means limited to this case. The obstruction of justice has become a pattern of our society: political-ly, with respect to campaigns and elections; legally, with respect to trials, the balancing of interests and the punishment sought for criminal acts; and in our daily lives, in the ways in which we have grown accustomed to simply lying. "Little white lies" are commonly accepted, rather than discouraged. Cheating has become rampant—as revealed, for example, in the scandals that have re-cently plagued some of our most respected educational, financial and athletic institutions. Misrepresentation and outright fraud have come to pervade our daily news media, in its coverage of every subject. Even candidates for the presidency of the United States have found it acceptable to cheat, hedge and lie about anything and everything that comes to mind. In such times, expedi-ency in obtaining a desired result appears to us to justify any means: we forget about doing what's fair and right, ethical and rational; we lie when we need to; we deceive as we feel it necessary; and in doing so, we obstruct justice in its purest sense.

To introduce the following discussion of the obstructions of justice specif-ic to the Casey Anthony case, however, we should define the term specifically. In Florida law, and throughout the jurisdictions of this country, "obstructing justice" is defined as "preventing witnesses from attending or testifying; sup-pressing evidence; and other acts defeating, impeding or delaying the admin-istration of justice, public or private, not constituting a distinct offense." Local laws in every jurisdiction generally prohibit such conduct as it interferes with the due administration of justice, as do the Federal Statutes; but it occurs with a far greater regularity than might be supposed, even on the part of governmental legal practitioners.

To take an example, one of the most basic violations or obstructions of justice is the effort to obtain a conviction through the use of false evidence. Such conduct is undeniably antithetical to the basic precepts of our Constitution. Yet the most glaring—and, unfortunately, frequent—instances of this are seen when the government itself, acting as the prosecution in a legal trial, is able to threaten witnesses (either directly or indirectly) to get them to change their testimony. I will be so bold as to say that there is not a single defense lawyer in this country who has not been aware of such instances, and of various other efforts on the part of prosecutors to pressure witnesses to deliver what the government has already decided should be the outcome of a trial. It is the proverbial attempt to shove a square peg into a round hole—and like many other obstructions that we will have occasion to point out in this book, it happens all the time.

The real tragedy is that this particular failing is, at bottom, a perfectly human one. We are all liable to believe in our own initial analyses of a situation, and are often tempted to adjust reality to suit our judgment rather than question the judgment itself. Law enforcement officers and legal professionals are as human as the rest of us; but when they fall victim to this temptation, and endeavor to create evidence to satisfy their predetermined judgment, rather than allow the real evidence to bring them to the truth, other human lives are at stake.

Complicating these matters is the unfortunate fact that justice, being all too often in the eyes of the beholder, is subject to distortions from outside as well as from within. In Casey Anthony's extremely well-publicized trial, and others like it, a secondary, though perhaps more insidious, source of obstruction arose in attempts by the media and other outside parties to adjust the story to fit their own predetermined notions and goals. Malicious prosecutors, self-serving politicians, self-aggrandizing talking-head lawyers and media opportunists made the trial an occasion to seek personal and financial gain by distorting the truth, fabricating allegations, reinforcing each other's empty testimonies with sound-bite lies and exaggerations, and pursuing many other questionable actions—all the while ignoring that a person's life was on the line.

One of the concepts most often expressed in our language is the question of whether a particular act or set of acts is "fair to one side or the other." Yet if a resolution is "fair," its fairness cannot be exclusively assigned to one side or the other—in order to be "fairness" it must be equitable. To argue that doing something or saying something was not fair to one person or another is inherently saying that it wasn't fair at all. In a trial, especially a murder trial, both sides require due process—the justice of a trial, from a legal perspective, isn't in a particular outcome being reached, but in its being reached by a process that is fair to both sides. By the end of this book's discussion of the Casey Anthony trial, I hope to have clearly demonstrated the many ways in which the prosecution and the news media were guilty of obstructing justice during that trial, in violation both of specific laws and of this general concept of "fairness"—of justice and morality in a basic sense.

Interestingly, during the drafting of this book there came to light a remarkable instance of obstruction of justice by a prosecutor, which exemplifies both the sort of misdoings it discusses, and their potential consequences.

On Friday the 19th of April, 2013, a former district attorney in Texas surrendered to arrest after a judge ruled that he had acted improperly during the prosecution in 1987 of a man accused of murder. The judge determined that the district attorney had failed to turn over material during the trial that would have helped to prove the defendant's innocence, which had resulted in the defendant's being convicted—and serving twenty-five years in prison—for a crime that he did not commit. The defendant was cleared by DNA evidence after serving that quarter of a century, during which time the prosecutor who had withheld the evidence had moved on in the legal community, and had himself become a judge.

The former district attorney-turned-judge was taken to trial on charges of criminal contempt, tampering with evidence, and tampering with government records. Ironically, the court ruling against him appointed a well-known criminal defense lawyer to act as his prosecutor. Now he himself had to worry about whether or not the famous defense lawyer leading the prosecution against him would reveal all of the evidence they held in order to ensure that he got a fair trial! From cases like these, we may draw hope that justice has a way of surviving even the vilest efforts to undermine it.

1

The Beginnings of Obstruction

That Cindy Anthony was as panicked and hysterical as she was when she made her famous call to the police is perfectly understandable. After all, she had not seen her grandchild for over a month, and felt that she was not getting straight answers from her daughter, Casey.

After pursuing and finally finding Casey, Cindy called the police. She told them that her granddaughter was missing and that her car, which she had recovered, smelled as though a dead body had been in it. At this, naturally enough, alarm bells went off. Deputies of the sheriff's office responded and confronted Casey. Eventually, after hearing her mother's accusations against her, the deputy sheriff on the scene decided to arrest Casey. Casey was handcuffed and placed into a marked sheriff's patrol car, in the backseat "cage," where she was held in the presence of several uniformed and armed deputy sheriffs, in several marked patrol cars.

Now, it is Law 101 in this country that when a suspect is taken into "custody" (meaning that they have involuntarily had their liberty suspended in being restrained), they are entitled to be advised of their legal rights before being questioned. This is a result of the landmark *Miranda v. Arizona* decision of 1966, when the United States Supreme Court declared that law enforcement cannot use any statement made by a defendant while in custody, nor use any developments from such a statement as evidence, unless the defendant has had certain rights—their "Miranda rights"—read to them, and signified that they understand them.

Casey Anthony was never read her Miranda rights that night. Though this became a very important point—and signifies to my mind the earliest instance of the sort of obstructive behavior that would characterize the State's handling of her case—I feel it is important to state in the beginning that the failure of a law enforcement officer to advise a suspect of his or her Miranda rights does not necessarily mean that the case will be dismissed. This is a misconception that seems to be somewhat pervasive among our citizenry. I cannot tell you how many hundreds of times I have had clients advise me, matter of factly, that their Miranda rights weren't read to them, hoping that this would result in a dismissal of the charges against them. To clarify the actual state of the case, a brief background is important.

Throughout the history of the recorded world, people have been subjected to many forms of pressure and coercion to make them do or not do things that they have had every right to do or not do as they see fit. As the law evolved in the United States, our founders created a Constitution in order to articulate these rights and legally counteract such forms of unjust coercion. Today, law enforcement officers, judicial officers, prosecuting attorneys and many other officials of the law swear an oath, in taking up their profession, that includes a promise to uphold this "supreme law of the land." Unfortunately, too many of those who swear this oath seem to be ignorant of the particular rights that the Constitution has been designed to protect. Among many others these include the provision, laid out in its Fifth Amendment, that no one can be compelled

2

to provide evidence or testimony against themselves; the right to counsel, stated in its Sixth Amendment; and the entitlement of all citizens, stated in the Fourteenth Amendment, to "due process of law."

The *Miranda* decision, which deals with all of these, has become almost daily vernacular in our country. It is cited and referred to constantly in television dramas and movies about criminal law issues—sometimes correctly, and sometimes with a great deal of literary license.

The decision arose out of an arrest in Arizona in 1963, when a man named Ernesto Miranda was arrested, charged with the very serious crimes of rape, kidnapping and robbery, and interrogated by law enforcement officers for several hours. During this questioning, the police alleged that he confessed to the allegations brought against him.

Later, it was revealed that Mr. Miranda had only an eighth-grade education, and a history of mental problems. He had no lawyer when he was questioned, and none was offered to him. At his trial, during which the district attorney's case was virtually entirely based on his alleged "confession," he was convicted and sentenced to a term of twenty to thirty years in prison. Appeals ultimately resulted in the case being brought to the United States Supreme Court, and in 1966 this court ruled in a series of cases—the first of which was *Miranda v. Arizona*—that any coerced or involuntary "confession" could not be used against a defendant unless he had first been advised of his right to remain silent and not provide testimony against himself (the Fifth Amendment) and his right to have an attorney to represent him during the process (the Sixth Amendment).

Ultimately, this decision was made in recognition of a much broader range of governmental abuses, which all too often had gone, and still go, unchecked. The old saying about being "rubber-hosed" had nothing to do with gardening; in fact, there have been innumerable cases in which defendants were beaten with hoses because it was thought that this would leave less evidence of abuse. Defendants have been treated to freezing temperatures without clothing; deprivation of water; refusal of the use of bathroom facilities; deprivation of food and sleep; and, in some more recent and sordid instances, waterboarding tortures. Yet as obviously reprehensible as these are, they are only the most extreme instances of governmental abuse, which, despite the precedent of Miranda rights, is much more widely prevalent in other forms.

Now again, the failure to read a defendant his Miranda rights does not in and of itself guarantee that the case against him will be thrown out. There are several other requisite conditions. First, and most generally, there has to have been some coercion in which the defendant was pressured into making statements that could be determined "incriminating." In other words, the defendant has to have had his or her liberty restrained to the point that a reasonable person would not have felt free to go at the time the police were interrogating them.

This can lead to a dangerously ambiguous ground in the processes of arrest and interrogation. It often happens that arrested defendants are scared, alone and uneducated, at least as far as the law is concerned; and skilled police take advantage of those weaknesses. Interrogations often include knowing and blatant lies by law enforcement, which, depending on the totality of the circumstances, can be considered completely acceptable.

Which brings us back to our case. That the arresting deputies did not advise Casey Anthony of her Miranda rights is a fact that has never been disputed. Casey did not have a lawyer present on the summer evening when she was surrounded by sheriff's deputies and hammered with accusations, nor was she ever told of the fundamental rights to which she, as a suspect in custody, was entitled.

What has been disputed, and will likely continue to be disputed, is whether or not she *was* in fact a suspect entitled to those rights at the time. Despite the circumstances of her arrest, the trial judge determined that she was not sufficiently in custody to have her rights read to her, a judgment that was later affirmed by the appellate court. A review of these circumstances, however, seems to dictate an opposite result.

After the young deputy had handcuffed Casey and put her in the "cage" of his police cruiser, he received radio communication from a detective who wanted the handcuffs taken off of her so that she could be questioned. The motive for this is clear: the detective, who would later become the lead investigator in Ms. Anthony's homicide case, wanted to be able to interrogate Casey without having to comply with the constitutional law of the United States. He knew that her being handcuffed clearly equated to her being "in custody," and thus entitled her to be advised of her Miranda rights: that she had a right to remain silent; that anything and everything she said could be used against her; and that she had the right to have a lawyer present. Not wanting such procedures to impede his questioning, the detective ordered the removal of her handcuffs under the assumption that she could be "un-arrested" in this way—even though the law does not provide for any such thing as an "un-arrest"—brought her inside the Anthony home, and proceeded to obtain a written statement from her.

This initial obstruction of justice was even more greatly aggravated later, when officers simply avoided telling the truth about it. A supervising detective who had been on the scene testified under oath—in a sworn deposition—that Casey had not ever been handcuffed. He knew that her being handcuffed equated unequivocally to a situation of "custodial interrogation," and that it would hurt "their case"—that is, the case they had already decided against her. Fortunately, the young detective who actually did the handcuffing told the truth—that he was ordered both to cuff and uncuff Casey. One might think that given such a clear testimony, no one could rationally attribute good motive to the police, or conclude that Casey was in fact not entitled to her Miranda warnings. We know now that none of this mattered in the eyes of the law.

The claim made by the prosecution was that, at the time of her questioning, and when she was asked to deliver her written statement, Casey Anthony was "free to go." Where and how she might have been expected to go is unclear. She was already in her home, with her parents, surrounded by law enforcement officers and with no ability to go anywhere. Certainly, people can differ in their interpretations and assign meanings to things that can astonish us with their variation. But would *anyone* conclude that a handcuffed and caged Casey was not under arrest, or that, surrounded by armed officers, she was in fact free to go? Isn't the notion that she might have voluntarily participated in such an investigation equally astonishing?

After Casey had been questioned late into the night, arrangements were made for her to meet with police again in the morning, about four or five hours later, and the detectives left to check up on some details she had given them.

During that first non-Mirandized interview at her family home, Casey had made statements about her work at Universal Studios and had begun to relate what would later be referred to as her "Casey world" story, about a fictitious nanny and her own alleged investigations into her daughter's disappearance. Now whether Casey had in fact been clearly competent at that time, or indeed living in a fantasy world of her own construction, is subject to fair debate. Yet one way or another, there is no question that the officials in charge of her case did what they did next in full awareness of what they were doing—and, I would argue, in defiant obstruction of justice.

Overnight, law enforcement obtained information from Universal Studios that Casey did not currently work there, as she had stated, but had been employed there some time previously. However, rather than confront Casey with the conflict upon meeting with her the following morning and there question her clearly and with straightforward motives—taking care to include an advisement of her constitutional rights—the police concocted a different scheme.

After a few hours of sleep, Casey was picked up by two detectives from the sheriff's department and driven some twenty miles from her home to Universal Studios. There the detectives and Casey met with Universal's head of security, who by now had become part of the detectives' plan. Casey and the detectives were checked in through security so that Casey could go to her (imaginary) office at Universal and show the detectives where she worked. One wonders how the detectives were able to keep a straight face, knowing they were playing such a game; but they did, walking with Casey some seven hundred feet down a sidewalk and around the corner to a building where she claimed to have an office. When they got there and started down the hallway, Casey stopped abruptly and confirmed that she didn't really work there.

At this point, Casey was led down the hallway into a small conference room barely larger than a billiard table—eight feet by ten feet with a small two-seat sofa and a chair—by three armed detectives. The door was closed and she was questioned vigorously for nearly an hour and a half, during which time she was repeatedly accused of various criminal acts. Despite her situation—a five-foot-two, 110-pound woman locked into a room with three 200-plus-pound detectives with guns—Casey Anthony was *still* never Mirandized; and later, during her trial, it was successfully maintained that she had *still* not been in custody at the time. As before, the detectives argued that they had told her she was free to go—an excuse that even the appellate court accepted. Yet as before, Casey had again been without the ability to go anywhere—and this time, twenty miles from home. It is difficult to see how she, or anyone else in such circumstances, could feel at all free to go.

Armed with the statements Casey had made at her home after being "un-arrested," and during their second "free to go" interrogation in the tiny room at Universal, the police now took Casey to the sheriff's department's headquarters, formally under arrest—as, despite their claims, she had in fact been before—and advised her for the first time of her constitutional right to a lawyer and right to remain silent. Unsurprisingly, when informed of these rights, she immediately invoked them.

In the initial stages of her legal proceedings, Casey's defense team filed a motion to suppress the evidence obtained from these non-Mirandized interrogations, and thereby prohibit the prosecution's benefiting from such flagrant violations of her constitutional rights. The court denied the motion, however, and allowed the evidence of these statements to be used in her trial. In addition to the serious offenses of first-degree murder, aggravated child abuse and aggravated manslaughter, Casey was also charged with four counts of lying to the detectives in her non-Mirandized statements. These charges were misdemeanors under Florida law, each punishable, at the time, by up to a year in the county jail and a $1,000 fine.

In response, the defense argued that Casey's "false statements" should not have been admitted because of the Miranda issue; that the statements were made in a continuous interrogation; and that, therefore, the rule of double jeopardy would prevent her from being constitutionally convicted on more than one count. Though these arguments again proved initially unsuccessful, this time the appellate court agreed with us in part, and reversed the trial judge. Finding that double jeopardy prohibited the multiple convictions for false statements, the court reversed two of the four counts; but by then, Casey had already served time for the wrongful convictions.

Strangely, however, even this miscarriage of justice didn't satisfy the state's vindictive appetite. Soon after this reversal, the Florida Legislature responded by passing a new law, under which making any false statement in connection with an investigation *specifically regarding a missing child* became a felony, punishable by up to five years in prison—as opposed to the "mere" one year for each count that Casey Anthony received. It is to be supposed that the state's present "law and order" legislative body would love to apply this law *ex post facto* to Casey.

It doesn't take much imagination or experience to anticipate that the same corrupt law enforcement attitude that intentionally failed to protect Casey's constitutional rights will do it again. The victims of such law enforcement conspiracies now face felony charges and lengthy prison times. What penalty, we might ask, would be appropriate for those law enforcement officers who knowingly and intentionally violate the constitutional rights of the citizenry they are sworn to protect? That is also a crime, punishable upon conviction, that can result in felony time in prison. But is such punishment likely to take place? Not in our lifetime, undoubtedly—unless and until the right (or rather, wrong) person is subjected, as Casey Anthony was, to such violations.

2

The Circus Begins

Once Casey Anthony had been arrested, it didn't take long for the sheriff's department to notify their "partners," the media. One can understand the need for a quick dissemination of news about a missing child, and no one can fault either the media or the sheriff's department for their first reactions in this regard. However, the purity of these initial intentions was very soon lost in the sea of secondary motivations and obstructive behavior that followed.

There was a time in this country, and even during my legal career over the past forty-three years, that the majority of newspeople were properly called by the name of "journalists." They were principled professionals who would report the news rather than try to create it. They served important functions in our society, disseminating information about wars, weather, the government and local matters of interest.

In our Constitution there is even a provision recognizing the value of that function: namely, the First Amendment. Going back again to the creation of our country, it was essential to the founding fathers that the American populace be guaranteed certain inalienable rights, such as the freedom of religion, the freedom of speech and the freedom of the press. These freedoms were deemed critical in preventing the outrageous consequences that arise from secret trials and hearings held in back rooms without the public knowledge; for prior to that, it had been common for people to be taken in the middle of the night and subjected to private interrogations, trials and punishments.

Even in modern times, we have seen fundamental lapses in regard for such basic freedoms. During the Second World War such secret "trials" happened frequently at the hands of the Nazis; and one might fairly argue that similar affronts are perpetrated against persons arrested in foreign countries and classified by our government as "enemy combatants." Yet notwithstanding these abuses—and judging by the way the public responds to them, for the most part—it is clear that the right to an open and public trial, candidly observed and reported on by news organizations, is a hallmark of free society.

Unfortunately, the good intentions of the authors of the Constitution, and the responsibility enjoined on those whose rights they had in mind, have been lost on many modern-day reporters. In our country it often seems today as though anything goes, as long as there is some economic benefit to be derived by it. The competition to be "first with the news" is observed every half hour on the half hour, on every television station in the country. Every news program wants to have the "exclusive" story, or "be first" to break it, even at the expense of full objectivity. In European countries such as Italy and England, lying broadcasters, deceptive publications and disingenuous "reporting" can be given civil penalties and, in some cases, criminal sanctions; but in America, there often doesn't seem to be any penalty for such misdoings. Nor is this lack of accountability made up for by a corresponding rigor in accreditation. There has never been any training or certification required for a person to become a journalist in our country; they need no educational degree, no professional license, no specific training. Nowadays it seems that the only requirement for the job is the willingness to say something sensational that might generate interest or response; and this is reflects a cultural change that I have seen in my lifetime.

Somewhere along the way, it seems—perhaps as a product of entertainment culture and the appeal of broadcast celebrity—the aspect of creditable reporting deteriorated. There can hardly be any dispute that the greater part of what newspeople do today is a far cry from simply reporting the news; they are now tasked to create it. Instead of stating facts and asking appropriate questions, the reporter's job is now typically a matter of sound bites, related to the commercial interest. A half-hour "TV show" in reality lasts only slightly over twenty minutes. The rest of the time is devoted to commercials, and the so-called news channels or news programs become more and more relegated to a position of commercial marketing—epitomizing the degradation of what is supposed to be journalism and fair reporting.

Since the drafting and redrafting of this book, a most remarkable incident has occurred that should shake our country's perception of its news media. In the wake of the Boston Marathon tragedy, reporters rushed to announce fictitious arrests, publish pictures of innocent suspects, and simply muddle the facts of the story—all for the sake of expediency in being "first with the breaking news." Shortly thereafter, many of them apologized for their incompetence; but they were hardly the first to behave in this way, and will not be the last.

Shortly after the first legitimate news went out about the missing Caylee Anthony, her home street, Hopespring Drive, was already inundated with news trucks and individual reporters' cars. Following Casey Anthony's interrogation at the sheriff's department, and subsequent jailing on the charge of child neglect, she was released on a bond and returned to reside with her parents, where she and they found themselves under constant observation by law enforcement and curiosity seekers alike. The street was effectively blocked in front of their residence, which soon became one of the top tourist destinations in Orlando. After thirty years of Disney World, Sea World and Universal Studios, the house on Hopespring Drive—where the media and its attendant populace gathered to chant, taunt and make references to the "baby killer"—was added to the list of Florida's top attractions.

How did this happen? Simply put, the news media had to keep a story alive. There was little interest in the story of a child having merely gone missing; such a story played too little upon the prejudices of the news audience and contained no dramatic element, no compelling antagonist. With the more complex narrative it was able to construct around Casey, the media now had an opportunity to keep the story alive and intriguing, day by day—even hour by hour. Worse still, having already bought into the same narrative, the sheriff's department stood by all the while, doing nothing to protect either the Anthonys or their innocent neighbors. Despite Florida law—which, like the law of every jurisdiction in the country, prohibits the crime known as "disturbing the peace"—the legions of police constantly present on Hopespring Drive took no preventive action.

Accordingly, people were attracted to the Anthony residence from all over the country—even, in some cases, at the sacrifice of planned vacations to the major attractions in Orlando. They came from Indiana, Michigan, Georgia, South Carolina and states even farther away; in hopes of being seen by their friends back home on television, they gathered en masse to chant slogans, and to accuse and taunt Casey, George and Cindy Anthony. The frenzied behavior of such uninvited participants often reached bizarre and shocking depths. One evening an angry mother, rushing to get in front of a camera and hurl insults at Cindy Anthony on air, slammed her car door on her own child's arm, ignoring even the child's screams of pain in her zeal. The sheriff's department, present as always at the scene, did nothing.

This, however, was just the beginning of the circus. From the summer of 2008 to December of that year, when Caylee's remains were finally found, there were demonstrations and processions constantly, day and night, in front of the Anthony home—and the news organizations loved it. They didn't have to get creative any more; or, for that matter, expend any effort searching for their news. All they needed to do in this case was sit on Hopespring Drive with the cameras and lights working and wait for the crowd to act out in any way it wished. Even *no news* was news in a case like this. No special knowledge was required, or facts needed, to perpetuate the forward motion of this dramatic media narrative; it moved itself by sheer imaginative force, and assimilated any facts that stood in its way. Not even the eventual verdict of the jury would slow its momentum; its conclusions had long since been settled. It had become an institutionalized concept, a brand, the "Case Against Casey."

I recall another case I defended years ago in which a defendant had been arrested on the allegation that there were illegal drugs in his house. This gentleman had no prior criminal history of any description whatsoever, in any jurisdiction. He was absolutely non-violent, and no one could legitimately suggest otherwise. He was simply a government employee who enjoyed smoking pot and playing backgammon with his friends at home from time to time. Regardless, law enforcement made the decision to arrest him in a violent home raid; and the first people they informed of this decision were the local news media.

Once all of the cameras were in place and rolling—and not before—SWAT officers began to smash against the door with a battering ram. Ironically, the door was one that opened out instead of in, so the ramming did nothing. Hearing the noise, the defendant opened the door to see what was going on.

He was immediately grabbed, thrown face-first onto the sidewalk, hit more than once and handcuffed, all with news cameras rolling in his face. Taking him to a patrol car, the police then allowed the news media to approach him one at a time and attempt to question him, hoping that he might make self-incriminating statements on camera without being officially interrogated. Unfortunately for them, the defendant—hurt, dazed and essentially in shock—had nothing to say; but the progression of attempted interviews continued for nearly half an hour before the media broke it off in order to rush to broadcast.

This level of involvement of the media in matters of law enforcement is growing more and more common. In many cases, such as the one I mention, it pushes the bounds of propriety. In such cases the needs of the media seem to be placed above those of suspects—who are, after all, innocent until proven guilty and deserve no more than anyone else to be subject to such sensationalist treatment. But there are other more extreme cases, in which the media's involvement actually impedes the due process of law to the extent that it comes to constitute an obstruction of justice in its own right.

The "Case Against Casey" was a case of this sort. Virtually from the beginning, the media was involved in her story—and influenced the behavior even of the legal professionals responsible for her life—to an unprecedented degree. The publicity spectacle surrounding the case would have been bad enough on its own; but the extent to which it was able to affect the innermost workings of the legal process itself, and override the objectivity of the law, was sobering even to one as experienced as myself.

Now, under Florida law, a defendant arrested for any charge other than a capital felony or felony punishable by life in prison is entitled to be released after being processed. Our Criminal Rules of Procedure outline a series of different levels of conditions for release in a matrix that is supposed to be followed by local courts.

The first and least restrictive of these conditions is a release of the defendant on his or her own recognizance. In plain English, this means the defendant is released on the condition that he or she promises to show up when ordered. Several lines below this is stipulated another condition of such release, namely, the posting of a surety bond. In this procedure, a bail bondsman puts up a bond, which is an insurance-like promise to pay a certain dollar amount in the event the defendant fails to appear. The defendant is often required to pay the bail bondsman a premium, as with all other insurance policies—this amount is usually ten percent, but is negotiable with the bail bondsman. This saves the defendant from needing to have the available cash on hand in order to get out of jail. Thus, if the bond is set at $5,000 or $10,000, the defendant calls a bail bondsman and arranges to pay him $500 to $1,000. The bail bondsman posts the bond with the court through the sheriff, and the defendant is immediately released from jail.

Casey's first arrest, after her interview at Universal Studios, was for the charges of child neglect and making false statements to the police. For virtually any other person similarly accused, the bond would have been $5,000, or *maybe* as much as $10,000. Only very rarely would it be any more than that. After all, Casey had no prior criminal record of any description, and there was no "glaring evidence" of her guilt. There was only media-generated hype and suspicion—but in this case, that proved just as influential.

Upon her arrest, Casey was taken before the first judge in her case, Mr. Stan Strickland. In these proceedings, instead of the routine bond to which any other similarly situated defendant would have been entitled, Judge Strickland ordered that her release require the posting of a $500,000 bond.

It is a fundamental assumption that an entitlement to bond be a reasonable one—one that the defendant in question would likely have the ability to post. An unemployed, 22-year-old woman is hardly likely to be able to post a half-million-dollar bond. Where would she get the $50,000 premium? More than one of the judges in the Orange County Courthouse confided to me that they had found this decision puzzling. Not only was it unfair, it unduly fed the media frenzy surrounding the case. It set Judge Strickland's official seal of approval on the suspicions already leveled at Casey, and ensured the continuation of the media's dramatization of her case. When a bail bondsman eventually did come forward to post her bond, he took care to engage in news conferences as he did—something I have never seen in my four-plus decades of defending criminal cases—and insisted publicly on having a guard stay with her 24/7. When Casey was bonded out, she was confined to her home and required to wear a GPS monitor on her ankle.

Interestingly enough, this was only the first indication of Judge Strickland's bias in the case. The transcript of proceedings would later reveal that the judge had effectively dismissed Casey as a liar out of hand. "The truth and Ms. Anthony are strangers," he is recorded as having said—despite the fact that he had not yet met Casey, and she had not been asked a question or said a word in court. Like so many other onlookers, Judge Strickland had formulated his opinion of Casey solely on the basis of the news media, and of the narrative it had already begun to generate.

While the search for Caylee Anthony was underway, and Casey Anthony, technically free on bond, was imprisoned by the media storm outside her parents' residence, the sheriff's department broadened their investigation in an attempt to reconstruct Casey's movements after the child had gone missing. They learned from friends and other investigating sources that she had gone shopping and engaged in other "normal" activities during the time that Caylee was missing, and were able to locate surveillance video of her shopping with a boyfriend. Eventually, they also learned that Casey had taken some checks from her (then) very good friend and had cashed them to buy certain personal items and do some general shopping. With pressure from law enforcement investigators, this "friend" was easily recruited as a "victim," and when the sheriff's department had obtained sworn statements from her regarding the loss of her checks and money, they proceeded to arrest Casey Anthony again.

At this point, Casey had a lawyer who could have been called and asked to bring her to the police station. Had the police made this request of him, he, like any lawyer, would have complied without difficulty. But instead, in consideration of the media circus outside the house on Hopespring Drive, the sheriff's department sent several marked patrol cars and numerous deputies rushing in to serve Casey her warrant and haul her off—for cashing bad checks. Given the level of drama the case had already reached, it was hardly surprising that even this act of dastardly "criminality" was sufficient indictment for most of the newspeople looking to validate their prejudgment of Casey, in whose view, it seems, it was hardly a leap from cashing a bad check to murdering one's own child. Yet the degree to which this informal indictment would affect her actual trial was something nobody could have predicted.

3

Spies, Lies, and Videotape

One of the first things that a citizen and potential defendant ought to know is that he has no right to privacy while in custody after being arrested. The police have the right to surreptitiously record everything he says and does inside a police cruiser; everything he says and does at the police station; and everything he says and does in jail. The only supposed exceptions to this are the conversations between him and a lawyer, and frankly, I don't believe in even that exception. I certainly don't think the police would ever overtly attempt to *use* conversations that occur between lawyer and client, but that does not mean they wouldn't record them.

During Casey Anthony's time in jail, she had visits from a number of people, including her mother, her father and her brother—all of which visits were videotaped and audiotaped without her knowledge. Her parents apparently knew this, and her brother certainly did. At the end of the day, Casey never made any incriminating statements, admissions or confessions during these unofficial interviews, but the sheriff's department tried hard to get her to.

George Anthony, Casey's father, had been approached by detectives early on in the case in an attempt to elicit his help as a spy. Again, the detectives wanted to circumvent Casey's Sixth Amendment right to legal counsel and interrogate her without her lawyer, Mr. Jose Baez, present. Deciding that they might be able to accomplish this with George Anthony's help, they met with George in the back of a patrol car and implied that by cooperating with them, he could clear his name from the speculations and rumors already circulating, that he was somehow involved in the death of his granddaughter. They instructed him to tell Casey to write a letter to her head warden, requesting to speak with the detectives in person. This would allow them to question her despite Mr. Baez's specific and unequivocal demand to the contrary, and without directly violating her constitutional right to counsel.

The plan almost worked. It was only foiled because a young lawyer working with Mr. Baez happened to visit Casey just before she was to be questioned and acted quickly to call off the detectives' interview. Their machinations, however, by no means stopped there. The same detectives also solicited Casey's brother to spy on her in the same fashion, even going so far as to work with him on a script to get her talking about the missing child. Lee did his best to get his sister to "slip up" and provide information as to Caylee's whereabouts, but was ultimately unsuccessful.

The interesting point here is that, like the "un-arrest" of Casey earlier, even these creative attempts to circumvent the law and Casey's constitutional rights are arguably just as illegal as the out-and-out violations they were contrived to avoid. It is true that Miranda rights, as per the Supreme Court's decision, apply only to custodial interrogations by law enforcement officers. But George and Lee were specifically approached by the police to act as interrogators on their behalf, and were provided with scripts and directions to that purpose—which made them agents of the police, and their participation in such counsel-free interviews glaringly illegal. It is undisputedly illegal for the police to send in an informant to pose as a suspect's cellmate in jail in order to obtain such information from him. How, then, is it acceptable for them to send in a blood relative with a script they provide in order to question a defendant? Yet despite lengthy hearings and arguments on the side of the defense against such behavior, the detectives were never officially reprimanded for it. It is fortunate that Casey Anthony had nothing to tell these de facto spies that could be used legally against her. Without a doubt, there are countless others in our legal system who are less fortunate.

Though the police recordings of Casey were not legally useful in the case against her, there was still a very meaningful channel open for their use in the obstruction of justice. Immediately after obtaining them, law enforcement officials turned these tapes over to the news media for use in their crusade to convict Casey in the public eye. Social networks and television stations around the country were soon hard at work on this new material provided them by the detectives, broadcasting selections from the tapes over and over, and using them as backdrops for speculative discussions and moral pontifications.

Some years back, the Florida legislature created a series of laws known as the Public Records Act, Florida Statute 119. The idea behind this act was simply to provide for public knowledge of what goes on in Florida legal proceedings. This sounds like a sensible intention on the face of it, but in its specific formulation, the act arms media agencies with an advantageous access to knowledge, with little or no restriction on how they use it. Under these laws, law enforcement is obligated to turn over whatever information a news agency requests of them, unless they elect not to by claiming that the information is part of an "ongoing investigation." A judge does not decide whether an investigation is ongoing or not, the police do—so if the police think the media will put the information to a use that is advantageous to them, they hand it over, and the media is free to use that information however it sees fit. Statements and images can be taken out of context and put to whatever purpose the media designates.

Now similarly, under the Florida Rules of Criminal Procedure—unlike in many other states—the prosecution, upon request, is obligated to provide the defense with not only the names and addresses of all potential witnesses, but access to *all* documents and tangible evidence that may be used in the case. This is particularly crucial in the state of Florida, where depositions can be taken of witnesses before going to trial. A deposition is when a witness—of any kind, law enforcement or civilian—is ordered by subpoena to come to the courthouse and be questioned, under oath, by the defense counsel in the presence of a court reporter, who permanently records every utterance that is made. Due to this advantage of pre-trial discovery—an advantage not granted by the federal court system—a significant percentage of criminal cases in Florida are resolved short of trial. Yet it necessitates granting the defense team access to relevant evidence much earlier on than in the federal court system, in which criminal defense lawyers are not permitted to take depositions at all, and evidentiary documents frequently aren't given to them until they are utilized in the trial itself.

In Casey Anthony's case, before the trial began there were some 26,000 pages of documents relating to the case. The news media were given access to every one of these documents, very often before the defense team was. On some occasions documents and papers would be handed to the media directly, but mailed to the defense—often on a Friday afternoon, so that the defense wouldn't have it until Monday, when the media would have had an entire weekend to speculate about the same information. I lost track of the number of times that I recieved phone calls over the weekend at my home or through my answering service to ask questions about discovery documents that I had not seen and knew nothing about.

This would seem to be a good thing, at least from the standpoint of public disclosure, but in this case, loaded as the media narrative around Casey had already become, it had an extremely negative consequence. By the time we went to trial, much of the evidence we would address in Casey's defense had already been given a prevailing negative spin in the news, affecting how it was perceived not only by the public audience, but even by court and legal officials; a bias which—as I will discuss in detail later on—the defense would find it extremely difficult to counteract.

4

How I Got into This Mess

Somewhere in my proverbially misspent youth, I seem to have been vaccinated with a need to assist the underdog. Perhaps because I was physically small as a young man, or because I was raised in economically deprived circumstances—to the point of being effectively homeless at the age of fifteen and on active duty in the United States Air Force at seventeen— the vaccination took. I don't like bullies; I am angered by people being taken advantage of due to their economic or other disadvantages; I am angered by governmental abuse of its citizenry at all levels.

I've had the honor to serve as the president of the Florida Association of Criminal Defense Lawyers, and for a decade as the Membership Chairman for the National Association of Criminal Defense Lawyers. These opportunities enhanced my awareness of, and concern for, other lawyers—particularly those being maliciously and wrongfully abused by news media and the courts themselves.

I have long thought that if there is one thing our society needs, it is a better-educated media. In my judgment, the best way to help create that is to try to assist the media in being accurate about what they report, and when I was more active with the local bar association, and committed to this thesis, I organized a group of lawyers and a committee specifically dedicated to dealing with the media. The idea was that there would be several lawyers who volunteered to provide information to the media, but would do so anonymously, without having their names and faces publicized. The goal was to give independent and objective legal advice to the media that they might use to increase their level of competence, without promoting commercial trade for individual lawyers. Within this program there were volunteers who specialized in divorce law, real estate law, wills and probate law—all civil and criminal fields. News agencies needing to know the law for a story or occurrence they were investigating would call a member of the committee and get a response that they could use with no byline for the lawyer.

For a while this practice worked well, but it was discontinued, ultimately for reasons of underutilization, which I can't but take for a sign of change in media priorities. Over the years, news media agencies have become less and less inclined to use such sources, I argue, not only because their emphasis has shifted toward other uses than the strictly observational, but because these sources require a much higher degree of involvement on their part, in checking facts and isolating the specific points in which the un-clarity lies. As deadlines have grown shorter and the race to get the news out first has intensified, there has been less time on the part of the industry for this kind of reasoned dialogue, and less patience on the part of the audience for its often complex evolutions. It is a true loss—however sanctioned by media consumers.

At any rate, early on in the "Case Against Casey," and before I was engaged directly by the defense, various local news-media personalities called me to ask questions about developments, motions and apparent strategies in the case. On each such occasion, I required that the reporters provide me with a copy of the motions or other papers filed that were behind their subject of interest so that I would have the opportunity to research any part of these questions and issues I might not already know about. The media called on me frequently in this capacity because of my known credentials with various bar associations, and also because of the hundreds of jury trials that I had conducted, many of which they had also reported on.

Ostensibly this was in order to more accurately inform the public, and for a while it went along very well. Yet even this stage of media involvement contributed to the public bias and affected the efficacy of evidence long before it came to be used in trial.

On one particular occasion, I agreed to appear in a televised interview, along with a prosecutor not involved in the case. We were in the studio preparing for this program when the (then) Orange County sheriff, Kevin Beary, who was also there to participate in a separate interview, hurriedly came into the area where I was. He said, "Cheney, they have found Caylee"—and excitedly using his hand and finger to gesture in a circular motion around his head, he explained that Caylee had been found with duct tape covering her entire head.

"Oh, my," I responded to him and the reporter, "if that's the case, then this investigation and mystery is about over." I explained that if in fact the child's head had been completely wrapped up with duct tape, there would be usable forensic evidence. There would likely be traces of fingerprints and DNA evidence. If the child had been poisoned, there would probably also be toxicology evidence from matter adhering to the tape. There might be skin, hair follicles, blood traces and so on. In such a case, I went on, there would almost certainly not be a trial, but rather a negotiated plea of some sort.

The disturbing thing about all this is that the sheriff's statement was based on misinformation to begin with. The chain-of-command report that he had heard was distorted and exaggerated: Caylee's head was not "wrapped" in duct tape at all. But beginning with our discussion of the forensic evidence that *might* have been obtained in such an event, the media's portrayal of this particular point gave it a slant that, by the time the "evidence" was brought up in court, it was much more difficult to dispel than it should have been.

One weekend morning, the *Orlando Sentinel* carried a big story, an exposé, about Jose Baez, then lead counsel for Casey Anthony, in which—for reasons I still don't know—the *Sentinel* reporter saw fit to seek to embarrass and disparage Mr. Baez. At the time, Jose Baez was not known to the public; he had not held positions with any associations or organizations; he wasn't a politician; he wasn't well known in the practice of law. Indeed, he had only been a member of the bar for a few years. Yet nonetheless, the newspaper decided to crucify him.

Now, at this point I had never met Jose Baez. I didn't know anything about him, and I doubt I would have recognized him anywhere but for the occasional glimpse on the TV news. I did know that he was a fellow defense lawyer and a member of my organization, and that he deserved fairer treatment than the *Sentinel* article had given him. Not only did I find the article outrageous and personally insulting to Mr. Baez, but I saw that it made no balancing mention of the prosecution in the case, or even of the history of its lead prosecutor, Jeffrey Ashton—whose own professional conduct in previous cases had been, as many lawyers knew, far from spotless.

I decided that this was just too unfair to be ignored, and I decided to help Mr. Baez. I spoke with an Orlando lawyer, a good friend of mine and a former president of the Florida Association of Criminal Defense Lawyers, who also knew that the appellate courts had reversed Mr. Ashton's convictions and chastised him for misconduct in other cases; and having researched some of these cases with his help, I sent the following letter to the *Sentinel* reporter, advising him that if he was going to write what he did, then in fairness he owed equal time and scrutiny to Mr. Ashton's history.

J. Cheney Mason, P.A.
Attorney and Counsellor at Law

* CRIMINAL LAW
  FAMILY LAW
  TRIAL PRACTICE-GENERAL

390 NORTH ORANGE AVENUE, SUITE 2100
ORLANDO, FLORIDA 32801
TELEPHONE (407) 843-5785
FAX (407) 422-6858

* FLORIDA BAR BOARD CERTIFIED
* NATIONAL BOARD OF TRIAL ADVOCACY CERTIFIED

May 7, 2009

Hank Curtis
Orlando Sentinel
633 N. Orange Avenue
Orlando, Florida 32801

Dear Hank,

     I read with interest your article about young Jose Baez and his personal background, both with the Bar and finances. I do not know Mr. Baez, but I have had dozens of occasions to comment on various aspects of the Casey Anthony case in the electronic media. I am not a fan. Having said that, I am also a senior criminal defense lawyer with almost forty years experience and think that there needs to be a balance and fairness in reporting about people involved in a case. I have been hoping that you would have a story to expose some of the background of Chief Prosecutor, Jeffrey Ashton, but I have not seen it. I gather, therefore, that you are unaware of his own history, which I suggest is far more important than young Mr. Baez.

     I am hoping that you will treat this letter as a confidential source of information and that you will take my leads to research them yourself.

     In beginning, you should know that the "policies" of the Appellate Courts generally include not making reference to the lawyers involved by name. There have, however, been circumstances in which the Appellate Courts have been confronted so many times with outrageous conduct and/or errors, be they malicious or negligent, that they then admonish the lawyers by name or simply mention their name in the Opinions. I and most of the senior members of the local Bar are well aware of the history of Mr. Jeffrey Ashton and the numbers of times that he has personally identified for errors and/or misconduct by the Appellate Courts.

     You may find some of the following of interest, and I hope you will follow through with them.

    A.   In 1991, the 5th District Court of Appeal reversed the conviction of Mr. Gerald Boyette specifically and directly because of improper comments made by Mr. Ashton and improper violation of the defendant's Constitutional Rights. In that case, the first trial ended in a mistrial, because of improper comments by Mr. Ashton. A second

---

trial resulted in a conviction, which was then reversed by the 5th District Court of Appeal because of improper argument by Mr. Ashton, both in his opening statements and closing arguments. The reported decision of this case may be found at 585 So.2d 1115, 1116 (5th District Court of Appeal 1991).

B.   In 2000, the Florida Supreme Court in the death penalty case of James Earnest Hitchcock wrote in its opinion that closing arguments of Jeffrey Ashton were error. Albeit the Court concluded that under the facts of this case the improper comments were "harmless error", the Supreme Court did mention Mr. Ashton by name on several occasions. The Court agreed that it was error but, as I said above, did not think it controlled the decision of the jury because of the overwhelming evidence. The Court did, however, go on to say, "we caution prosecutors to adhere to the statement in the standard jury instruction which explains that mitigating circumstances are...". They specifically further held that it was erroneous for the prosecutor (Ashton) to say that the circumstances [regarding the Defendant's poverty and living circumstances] are not mitigating. This case may be found at 755 So.2d 638, 642 (Florida 2000).

C.   Again, in 2004, the Florida Supreme Court was compelled to reference Mr. Ashton by name in the case of John Steven Huggins. You may recall that Mr. Huggins kidnaped, robbed, and murdered Carla Larson in Orange County in 1997. The trial was held in that case, after change of venue to Duval County in 1999, and Mr. Huggins was convicted and, ultimately, sentenced to death. However, shortly thereafter, defense counsel learned that Mr. Ashton had withheld information that he should have represented to the defense in accordance with U.S. Supreme Court dictates in *Brady v. Maryland*. Mr. Huggins filed a Petition of Writ of Habeaus Corpus and Mr. Huggins was granted a new trial, specifically because of the violations of the prosecution in the case. In page 767 of that Opinion, the Court discussed Mr. Ashton's failure to disclose "Brady" material during the first trial. Mr. Huggins thereafter attempted to disqualify Mr. Ashton because of his Brady violation, but was unsuccessful. The important part is that the Court confirmed without question that the new trial of the lengthy Huggins case was necessitated directly because of Jeffrey Ashton's conduct.

D.   More recently, Mr. Ashton was referenced and criticized in the case of *Cancel v. State*. Here, the 5th District Court of Appeal made reference to the fact that Mr. Ashton had improperly objected to a jury instruction on self defense, which objection was overruled by the Judge. Apparently, however, Mr. Ashton was successful in brow-beating the Judge into changing her mind and giving an improper instruction. The end result, however, was that the conviction was upheld, again, on the concept of "harmless error" to which there was a vigorous descent. See *Cancel v. State*, 985 So.2d 1127 (5DCA 2008).

May 7, 2009
Page Three

I do not claim that this is an exhaustive list, but I know of no other attorney, prosecution or defense, that has had his/her name so frequently made prominent by the Appellate Courts because of misconduct. I wonder how much the first Huggins case cost the taxpayers? The same with Boyette?

While I have no personal knowledge, I think that (based on a tip to me) you might want to investigate bankruptcy filings as to Mr. Jeff Ashton. Since you did such an expose on Mr. Baez about finances, this might also be grounds for further "fairness".

Sincerely,

J. Cheney Mason

JCM:kdm

As a side note, it may not prove surprising that to this day, neither the reporter nor the *Sentinel* has printed a word about the facts contained in my letter regarding Mr. Ashton's history. One wonders if, had that been done, it would have been as easy for Mr. Ashton to be elected chief prosecuting attorney for Orange and Osceola Counties, even after losing the Casey Anthony case and "retiring" from the State Attorney's Office in order to run for that position.

In any event, when he found out about my letter, Mr. Baez was very grateful for my concern. He began routinely calling to ask me questions about strategy and law, and to seek help in defending Casey. This got to be so frequent that finally, one day sitting in my office, I looked him in the face and asked him if he was trying to enlist me to help him try the case. His answer was yes. *Oh boy*, I thought, *now I've done it.*

Based on my knowledge at this point, and taking into account the many complicated aspects of Florida and federal law, I believed that Casey Anthony's was not going to be a death-penalty case. I also anticipated that if a trial did take place, it would be of relatively short duration—likely lasting no more than a couple of weeks. Little did I know that the State would not in fact produce *any* of the evidence they had so far tried to convince the world they possessed and that, having initially made the humane decision to waive pursuit of the death penalty, they would later change their minds and reinstate the death penalty as their goal for the trial.

Yet had I known any of this, I would still have come to the conclusion I did—that I could not in good conscience turn down the case. I have handled several dozen homicide cases in my career—some well noted in the public records and media, and others with limited media attention—and I knew, from the conversation with Mr. Baez forward, that given the chance, I would agree to join the defense team. Ultimately, however, the decision had to be Casey's.

When I met with Casey Anthony for the first time, she had already endured several months of destructive media attacks. Mysterious and conflicting stories concerning the discovery of her child's remains had completely saturated the media, some of which she had been exposed to through the television in the jail's dayroom. Most of this, however, she was spared, as— ostensibly for her protection—she was jailed in isolation lockdown the entire time. Casey Anthony would ultimately spend almost three full years locked in a small, single-person cell, twenty-three out of twenty-four hours a day, during which her only reprieves were when she was being interviewed by a member of the defense team. With all of my experience, I cannot begin to understand or describe what a horror that had to have been for her.

The evening I met Casey in the jail dayroom—we went at night, to avoid media attention—I was initially shocked at how small she was. She is indeed a tiny person; her little wrists are about the size of two of my fingers. At the time, at just barely over five feet tall and perhaps 100 or 110 pounds, she seemed almost a child herself—albeit one, as it turned out, with the courage of a lion.

Jose introduced me to her, and she smiled with a broad, beaming happiness and a bright alertness in her eyes. She had apparently already heard some things about my reputation and was very excited and pleased that I was there. Reminding her that I did not necessarily trust the sanctity of the so-called claim to privacy for attorney-client interviews, I steered the conversation toward a general discussion of her and her educational background. I wanted to try to determine a few basic points that I typically look into in the beginning of such cases—including whether or not she was psychologically stable. I wondered how she had weathered the barrage of media accusations, assaults, and public indictments and convictions thus far, in addition to her legal ordeal.

During this first meeting we didn't discuss the fact of her guilt or innocence. I was interested in meeting her as a human being and in putting a face on the person from all the stories. I had seen her on television innumerable times by then; but now, even in the jail setting, I couldn't help but be impressed by her personality, warmth and strength. She maintained a politeness that one could hardly have expected under those circumstances and was very appreciative of my willingness to help her.

I too am thankful that I made the decision to join her defense, and that I was supported by my wife and colleagues in doing so. Even through so difficult a case, and with so many obstacles to overcome, Casey Anthony was a delight to represent. That she was able to endure the confinement and criticism she did is a tribute to her inner character.

5

Now What?

Recall that in Florida law, the defense has the distinct advantage of being able to question witnesses before trial in a process known as deposition. The State is required to provide defense attorneys with all of the names of its witnesses, as well as to identify and provide access to all tangible evidence within fifteen days of a request by the defense. Most often, the State is very cooperative in this process, and in allowing additional time to work with the defense.

Now that I was on this case, I intended for it to be handled properly. After forty years' experience and the handling of quite a few homicide cases, I knew how I wanted to work in order to get the job done effectively. I had seen some of the unfair advantages held by the prosecution in previous cases and was determined to work as efficiently as possible in order to keep the deck stacked as evenly as possible. Yet even I was unprepared for the degree of obstruction we would encounter in defending this case.

The State had already provided "partial discovery" by listing a number of witnesses that they intended to call upon during the trial. In order to expedite the deposition of these witnesses, Florida rules require witnesses to be categorized by the State as either A-, B- or C-category witnesses. "A" witnesses are those witnesses who are inherently relevant to the case at hand—whom the State definitely intends to call as witnesses in the trial, and whose depositions the defense is automatically entitled to take. "B" witnesses are those who *may* be called during the trial—whose testimony is seen as only moderately relevant to its outcome—and can be deposed upon special agreement with the prosecution, or by a court order. "C" witnesses are only distantly related to the case, are not intended to be called during trial at all, and so are not subject to deposition.

In this case—and for all too many cases prosecuted in this jurisdiction—the State Attorney's Office, for reasons known best to themselves, did not categorize their witnesses separately in this fashion. They simply categorized all of them as "A" witnesses. This, they claimed, was because they didn't want to realize later that they had made a mistake in determining whether or not the proper witnesses were disclosed and could be used; but truth be told, it was because they didn't want to go to the trouble of separating witnesses, or to be held accountable for their classification. Indeed, I have found few jurisdictions in the state of Florida in which prosecutors are professional enough to review their cases before filing and categorizing witnesses.

What this meant for the defense was that the witnesses had to be brought to the courthouse to be questioned in order to determine what their testimonies might be and of what real value they were to either side. This requires coordination with the state attorney so that both groups of lawyers can have the fair opportunity to be present, and it also requires a lot of money. Attorneys have to pay a court reporter to be present at every deposition, who generally charges a per-diem fee of $85.00 or more, simply to appear. If what is said is deemed important enough to be typed up, they charge $4.25 or more per page. Thus, when a defense lawyer or the State wants to memorialize the testimony given in a deposition, it can quickly get very expensive. Moreover, expert witnesses have to be paid their fees and expenses, which are sometimes shockingly high; and any additional investigation—by the defense, at any rate—requires hiring private investigators. The prosecution's investigation, of course, is already being carried out internally, and since the prosecution functions as an arm of the State, all of their other expenses are taken care of by taxpayer dollars. On the side of the defense, the money has to come from somewhere else—the client, his or her supporters or the lawyers themselves.

In our case, there was no money—or rather, what there was had been depleted before I joined the case. Mr. Baez had evidently sold some photographs of Casey to one of the major news networks for $200,000; he had also obtained a private contribution—$75,000, I'm told—from a lawyer who was at one time involved in the case. Yet this money was gone by the time I came on, with no prospects of more coming in.

I had already agreed to take the case pro bono, even knowing it was going to be a battle. It would surprise me, in the end, to see just how much time and money it took to defend Casey's life; by closest estimate, my unbilled hourly time alone amounted to close to a million dollars—not including the many tens of thousands of dollars in expenses paid out-of-pocket. But to be thwarted from the beginning by lack of funds was extremely frustrating. Right when I came on, I was faced with an ugly choice: either accept the inability to take depositions and investigate the case properly, or try to find some other resource.

Upon obtaining the witness list—which comprised then, as I recall, 125 or more names—I realized we were already far behind schedule in the deposition process. Only a very few depositions had been taken, and those only partially. In a death penalty case, this simply wouldn't do.

I had worked with Linda Drane Burdick, the formal lead counsel for the prosecution, on several prior cases, and knew her to be a professional and honorable person. We had a meeting to discuss moving forward with our very heavy deposition schedule, during which I asked Linda if she would go to the trouble to more adequately categorize the long list of "A" witnesses, so we could avoid wasting time in taking the depositions of witnesses with only a peripheral involvement in the case. She agreed, but unfortunately, she didn't do it in the end. Knowing Linda and her history, I couldn't but suspect that it was others on the prosecution team who had objected to her carrying out what she had told us she would do. One way or another, though, we were left with no money and potentially more than a hundred costly depositions to take.

There is a procedure that I have successfully undertaken in similar circumstances in the past that I decided to invoke in this case. We filed a motion to have Casey Anthony declared indigent. Under this motion, if the court agreed that she was so, the State of Florida would pay the cost of investigations, depositions and expert fees for the defense.

Having filed our motion, we scheduled a hearing before Judge Strickland. Ordinarily such a hearing is a perfunctory, non-interesting proceeding that nobody would take note of. But not in this case; this was Casey. The result: a courtroom full of news media, with an army of television trucks and crews around the courthouse and curiosity seekers cramming themselves in at every door. This may have been seen only as a nuisance, but in light of the exceptional scene that followed, one may suppose it to have been obstructive to a deeper degree.

It is important to point out here that, regarding a criminal trial, the prosecution really has no "stake in the fight" over funding. The State Attorney's Office has its own separate and independent budget amounting to millions of dollars. They also have an unlimited source of investigators and experts available to them. In our case, they had the FBI, the Florida Department of Law Enforcement, the Orange County Sheriff's Department, the Orlando Police Department, the Metropolitan Bureau of Investigation, the state attorney's own investigating staff, and every federal law enforcement agency in the country on call—at any time, for any purpose.

Nevertheless, at the indigence hearing for Casey Anthony, in the overwhelming presence of the news media, the prosecution objected to our motions, to the point of cross-examining Mr. Baez regarding the funds he had already spent. They asked the defense team generally, and Jose Baez specifically, if there were any book deals, movie deals or other such projects in the works that could provide us with funding, which, of course, there were not. Though there was no evidence whatsoever to contradict what we were saying, even the judge continued to be skeptical, and at one point I found myself simply asking him, "You trust me, don't you?" Recognizing my standing, he finally agreed, and allowed us to submit a private accounting of the money that Mr. Baez had received. Soon thereafter, Casey Anthony was declared indigent.

Now it seemed the defense would at least have some small ability to level the playing field. Yet there was another state agency to deal with, which would prove susceptible to the same obstructionist tendencies.

The Justice Administrative Commission is a commission, personified by a single lawyer, that decides whether or not to pay requested expenses for the defense. Even when the judge approves the propriety of expenses for witnesses or assistance in a case, the JAC frequently oppose it, sometimes to the point of absurdity. They have, for instance, guidelines by which the amount to be paid for a private investigator is limited to $40 per hour, despite the fact that the average investigator's rate is three times that or more. Likewise, they restrict the amount of money to be paid to court reporters in depositions, both for their time and for their transcription work.

This is one of the points in which obstruction seems to be built into our legal system. The State prosecution has no such commission, or even tax-watch organization, looking over their shoulder; nor do they have to restrict their spending in accordance with any such guidelines. Their travel and access to witnesses—perhaps even to expert witnesses—is completely unfettered. In our case, their hotel bills, their meals, their taxis and their flights were all paid for, as were all fees and expenses for their expert witnesses. There was no need for them to ask the judge's permission, or to send a bill for approval; they just spent what they needed to spend. The defense had to beg for every dime—and were frequently denied.

This form of obstruction through economic constraints would be manifested throughout the rest of the proceedings. When Mr. Baez asked the court to pay to provide the defense with a jury consultant—of which the prosecution already had at least one—the judge responded, "Mr. Baez, you've got Mr. Mason. He's been doing it for forty years. You don't need an expert." When we wanted to take the deposition of one of the State's so-called expert witnesses, we would have to pay the travel expenses to get to them. When we traveled to take the deposition of a witness in Knoxville, Tennessee, I paid for our flights, the taxes, the hotel and all other expenses related to travel. One of our team had to participate via phone, rather than incur the additional travel expense. The state prosecutor, Mr. Ashton, showed up there on the state attorney's budget, accompanied by his own consulting expert, a professor from the University of Florida. When it came time to go to trial, the defense team had to pay all of our travel and accommodation expenses during the two weeks required for jury selection in Clearwater. The State's entire entourage traveled there on taxpayer money.

It doesn't pay to be a poor defendant in this country to begin with. But besides the unfair financial advantage that our system grants to State prosecutors, its ordinary restriction of defense funding to private sources leaves open another avenue for obstructive media influence. Poorer defendants often rely on external contributions to fund their cases; and, in the case of defendants like Casey Anthony, whom the media decides to vilify early on, such external contributions dry up very quickly. How can one be expected to drum up such necessary resources, financial or otherwise, from a public, or even from friends and family, that have been persuaded of their guilt from the beginning?

The converse, it's worth pointing out, is just as applicable, and defendants of very questionable standing have received disproportionate amounts of financial support from private contributors, practically sight unseen, for the same prejudicial reasons. Long before the circumstances of Trayvon Martin's death were known, George Zimmerman was given huge amounts of money by the National Rifle Association to support his acquittal for the shooting—simply on the basis of his public presentation as a gun-rights avatar. In this type of case as in the other, media involvement too easily affects trial conduct and takes it quickly out of the realm of what most Americans would consider "due process," and into that of straightforward obstruction.

6

Blog This! There Goes the Judge

The judge initially assigned to Casey Anthony's case, Stan Strickland, enjoyed a substantial reputation among the lawyers as being a fair-minded and easygoing judge. By whatever luck of the draw, I had never handled a criminal case before him, but only civil cases such as divorces. Still, I was aware of Judge Strickland's reputation and his personality, and before I became involved in Casey Anthony's defense, I had every reason to think highly of him.

The Central Florida chapter of the Florida Association of Criminal Defense Lawyers has conducted judicial polls for many years. These polls began some time ago, when I was the president of this chapter. The goal was to provide a system by which judges might be fairly appraised as to their knowledge, demeanor, character and overall performance. The relative ratings were then distributed to the judges so they could see for themselves how they compared with their colleagues. Many of us, including senior lawyers, would then make appointments to meet with certain of them for off-the-record, professional conversations, during which we would inform them of specific criticisms that had been brought against them by lawyers in the polls, and thus initiate improvement in the system by feedback. Most judges received this information constructively and made efforts to improve.

Unfortunately, after a few years of this productive process, some of my colleagues began to include personal attacks and epithets against some judges. Apparently some of the lawyers had not obtained the results they wanted and had blamed it on the judge—always an easier recourse than owning up to one's own shortcomings or accepting the facts as they are. It got to the point that some of the "comments" being added to the polls were more than just scandalous, unprofessional and immature; yet notwithstanding our objections to the new generation's methods, the younger lawyers espousing their right to criticize in this destructive way outnumbered the rest of us. The insulting, incompetent and unfair criticisms not only continued, but became more and more prevalent. I quit participating in such judicial polls myself, as did most of the senior lawyers, a very long time ago for this very reason.

Through all this, Judge Strickland had continued to receive high marks, consistently scoring at or near the top with the young lawyers. It seemed to many local lawyer observers that Casey Anthony was lucky to have drawn Judge Strickland for her case.

This honeymoon didn't last long, however, given the circumstances of the bond hearing; when, as I mentioned earlier, the judge dismissed Casey as a liar despite not having had any evidentiary hearing on the subject, or hearing her testify at all. Other motions on the part of the defense seemed to be denied spontaneously, with little thought or consideration given to them beforehand; and when I joined the team, they confided in me several of the major concerns they had had prior to my involvement in the case. Given the status of Judge Strickland with the bar, and how well he had fared in the evaluation polls, I was quite surprised; but the surprise ended a bit later, when I was informed by Mr. Baez about a particular blog site that Judge Strickland turned out to be reading and referencing.

At the time it came up I had never seen, heard about, discussed or participated in the Internet world of anonymous criticism and statements known as blogs. So when I learned what the blogs were saying about Casey in this case, I was appalled. I find it remarkable that citizens of our country feel entitled to go on the Internet and criticize any person about anything they wish, without any regard to merit, thought or intelligence; but it seems that one person behaving badly creates another, and soon that behavior passes for normal, without any form of punishment or sanction. Certainly their anonymity grants them a greater degree of impunity than they deserve.

Every judge knows how distorted the news media is, in virtually every circumstance. Accordingly, a judge sitting on any case knows that, as ubiquitous as the news is, it is highly inappropriate for him to dwell on, or attribute any special credibility to, any particular news story published about that case.

In this case, there was a blogger whose work had apparently caught Judge Strickland's eye. This blogger was not a lawyer; had no legal training; and like all journalists, held no professional accountability whatsoever for what he had to say—even, in this case, for the hatred he engendered. Among the pieces of fine, objective reporting he ran on his site were articles with such headlines as "Casey Guilty As Charged" and "Casey Must Die." Not only did he seem to have a great deal of energy to spend in infecting the Internet, but he also frequently showed up in court as one of the regular curiosity-seekers. It would be hard, I would imagine, for any person with a modicum of sensibility and awareness of fair play to believe what was being blogged about the "Case Against Casey"—but then, so many of us seem to thrive on secondhand gossip disguised as information.

One day after a hearing, when all of the lawyers for both sides had left the room along with the courtroom mob, the television camera recording that day's events was left running. Whether or not Judge Strickland was aware of this fact is known only to him; but personally, I doubt it.

What the film shows is the courtroom, empty but for the sheriff's deputy at the door, as the last of the observers are being escorted out. At some point, the ominous voice of Judge Strickland is heard to say to the deputy, "I want to talk to that man. Ask him to come back in."

"Who?" the deputy asks.

"The gentleman there, in the blue-and-white checked shirt," replies the judge.

The deputy points to the gentleman in question and says, "Him?" The man turns around, shocked and obviously surprised about what is going on. He clearly doesn't understand. "Yes," the judge says. "Bring him back in here."

The courtroom observer—the blogger I have mentioned—is escorted to the bench. Though the camera does not show Judge Strickland's face, his voice is very clear in the recording. He engages the blogger in a short conversation, during which the judge tells him what a good job he thinks the blogger is doing; how fair and accurate he is; how much he, Judge Strickland, enjoys reading his blogs; and so forth.

Now there's no doubt that this was shocking to the blogger, but it was devastating to our team. Not only was Judge Strickland already invested in the hatred campaign against Casey—he was evidently so invested in it as to have gone out of his way to seek it out. His exposure to these blogs could not have been accidental, as it might have been with a story in the papers or on television; it would have required intentional computer research on the subject—and a penchant for gossip.

After confirming the facts, I discussed the issue with the defense team. My question was, "Why hasn't something been done about this?" The answer lay in the team's lack of experience and uncertainty as to what to do. Fortunately, I had no hesitation in taking action. In my forty years of practice prior to this situation, I had only felt the need to file a motion to disqualify a judge on two other occasions, but it was clear that this was a case that called for such action. In reviewing the precedent cases relevant to the procedure, I found few circumstances of judicial misconduct quite as outrageous as this. It was clear that we could not, in professionalism or good conscience, sit by with a young woman facing the death penalty and allow a judge with such obvious disdain for his duty to remain on the case.

After having determined to file a Motion to Disqualify—but before filing it—I asked to approach the bench to talk to the judge off the record. The prosecutors accompanied me, whereupon I told the judge that I needed to talk to him privately, away from the public eye, and suggested that we all go into the back office. I had neither the need nor the desire to hurt or embarrass him through formal comments; I simply wanted him off the case. I saw no reason not to give the judge a fair and private opportunity to remove himself from the case and avoid the embarrassment of an otherwise required pleading. Judge Strickland, however, refused even to speak to us in private. His response to my request was, "We can't do that. Look at all of the cameras and media here. What will they think?" This confirmed the necessity of our motion, so we went ahead and filed it.

The issue was so critical to the case, and to a comprehensive review of the flagrant obstructions of justice in it, that I am reproducing here the entire Motion to Disqualify and Memorandum that we filed to have Judge Strickland recused. The name of the blogger and his screen name are redacted; because, while I disagree with his philosophy and the opinions he espoused, he was in no way the source of this outrageous misconduct.

IN THE CIRCUIT COURT OF THE NINTH JUDICIAL CIRCUIT
IN AND FOR ORANGE COUNTY, FLORIDA

STATE OF FLORIDA,

Plaintiff,

v.

CASEY MARIE ANTHONY,

Defendant.

_____/

CASE NO.: 48-2008-CF-0015606-O
DIVISION 6
Hon. Stan Strickland

DEFENDANT, CASEY MARIE ANTHONY'S, AMENDED MOTION
TO DISQUALIFY TRIAL JUDGE
(amended as to correct notary)

COMES NOW the Defendant, CASEY MARIE ANTHONY, by and through her undersigned attorneys, Jose A. Baez, Esquire and J. Cheney Mason, Esquire, and, pursuant to Florida Rule of Judicial Administration 2.330, moves this Court to disqualify himself, and shows:

1. The Defendant, CASEY MARIE ANTHONY, reasonably fears that she will not receive a fair trial because of the conduct and apparent prejudice and bias of the judge, the Honorable Stan Strickland, because of the following reasons:

a. The precipitating grounds for disqualification is the revelation that the judge has apparently developed a personal relationship with a journalist/blogger known fictitiously as [name redacted], who has historically presented numerous stories of severe bias and prejudice against the Defendant. The revelation of the involvement between the judge and the journalist, [name redacted], includes the fact that recently the judge, learned of said journalist's illness, apparently from a blog, and thereafter, in some method or manner, learned the journalist's phone number and said judge thereupon called the journalist to express his personal concern for his well-being. This relationship was not disclosed to counsel for the Defendant until said journalist was interviewed by an investigator working for the defense on Sunday, April 11, 2010. Said revelations made by [name redacted], confirmed the truth of various statements made by the judge to said journalist and blogs posted by the journalist. This discovery was within ten days of the filing of this Motion for Disqualification, as required by the aforesaid Rules of Judicial Administration.

b.   The gravamen of the statements and the prejudice created results from Judge Strickland at a judicial proceeding in this case apparently recognizing the face of the journalist and requested the said journalist approach the bench. At that time the judge essentially validated the journalist's opinions and blogging actions by telling said [name redacted] how he (the judge) admired [name redacted] and thought him to be fair, posting the best blogs that he had read on the internet.

c.   Examples of the blogs written by journalist [name redacted] that the Court apparently approved of and validated included such titles as: "Casey Anthony must die!" (April 20, 2009); "Caylee's murder: Premeditated and pretty stupid, too" (February 1, 2009); and "Guilty as charged" (June 23, 2009). Copies of said blogs are attached hereto as "Exhibit A", "Exhibit B", and "Exhibit C".

d.   These specifically titled blogs and numerous other pro-prose-cution assertions were posted by [name redacted], a/k/a [name redacted], prior to the judge's statements of how fair he thought [name redacted] was, etc.

e.   The approval by Judge Strickland of [name redacted] blogs is incomparable and chilling at a minimum as to the Defendant's expectation of a fair trial.

f.   [name redacted] has also been interviewed by investigators working for the prosecution and may well be a witness in this case.

2.   Defense counsel, in an effort to ascertain the facts of postings by [name redacted] and involvement with said website prompted under-signed counsel to have investigator, [name redacted], locate and interview [name redacted]. Said interview occurred on Sunday, April 11, 2010, with a subsequent phone call between [name redacted] and [name redacted] on the following day, Monday, April 12, 2010.

3.   The Affidavit of investigator [name redacted], together with a transcript of the recorded interview with [name redacted], is attached here-to as "Exhibit D" in support of this Motion.

4.   The cumulative effect of this recent revelation of the judge's activities and relationship with blogging, when considered in light of nu-merous other challenged statements of the Court, demands disqualification of this Court.

5.   Attached hereto is a Memorandum of background and law in this case culminating, with the recent discovery of revelations as set forth above, establishing absolutely clear and compelling support for the fear of the Defendant, CASEY MARIE ANTHONY, in that she cannot receive a fair trial before this judge.

J. CHENEY MASON, ESQ.
One of the attorneys for Defendant

IN THE CIRCUIT COURT OF THE NINTH JUDICIAL CIRCUIT
IN AND FOR ORANGE COUNTY, FLORIDA

STATE OF FLORIDA,

Plaintiff,

v.

CASEY MARIE ANTHONY,

Defendant.

_____/

CASE NO.: 48-2008-CF-0015606-O
DIVISION: 16
Hon. Stan Strickland

**MEMORANDUM IN SUPPORT OF DEFENDANT'S MOTION
TO DISQUALIFY TRIAL JUDGE**

COMES NOW the Defendant, CASEY MARIE ANTHONY, by and through her attorneys, Jose A. Baez, Esquire and J. Cheney Mason, Esquire, and respectfully submit this Memorandum in Support of her Motion to Disqualify Trial Judge, and shows:

STATEMENT OF FACTS

1.   CASEY MARIE ANTHONY was arrested on July 16, 2008. The charge was Child Endangerment, a Third Degree Felony, and Making False Statements to Law Enforcement.

2.   Soon after Miss Anthony's arrest, her case became a national media-driven phenomenon featuring extensive coverage in both local and national media outlets.

3.   The Honorable Stan Strickland, Circuit Judge, was assigned to Miss Anthony's case. On July 22, 2008 Judge Strickland conducted a bond hearing and set bail for Miss Anthony on the Third Degree Felony and misdemeanors of five hundred thousand dollars ($500,000.00). During that proceeding, the judge, on the record, stated that "...the truth and Miss Anthony are strangers". Miss Anthony had not testified in any capacity.

4.   At Miss Anthony's bond hearing, Judge Strickland further stated that it was Miss Anthony's Constitutional Right not to speak, yet, in the same hearing, the judge stated "and normally she would be entitled to a reasonable bond...[but] not a bit of useful information has been provided by Miss Anthony".

5.   Judge Strickland referred one of Miss Anthony's attorneys to the Florida Bar for disciplinary investigation based upon an untrue hearsay statement of an investigator at that time hired by the Defendant's parents, which statements, even if true, was entirely legal and did not constitute grounds for disciplinary action. The attorney was cleared by the Bar Association.

6.   Judge Strickland has made off the record comments to both the prosecution and Miss Anthony's defense lawyers that he (the judge) would like to wait until after his reelection is over to set the trial in Miss Anthony's case. Such action reveals the judge's concern about politics and is a violation of Canon 2 of the Code of Judicial Conduct.

7.   In November of 2008, [name redacted], also known as [name redacted], began writing posts about Miss Anthony and her case on his blog, "[name redacted]". By January of 2009, eleven out of [name redacted] fifteen posts during the month were about Miss Anthony's case. See [name redacted], "Entries from January, 2009", [name redacted], "Available at [name redacted]."

8.   On October 19, 2009, [name redacted] posted an entry on his blog describing an encounter he had with Judge Strickland after a Motions hearing in Miss Anthony's case that [name redacted] attended on October 16th. See [name redacted] "It was my honor, your pleasure...", [name redacted], available at [redacted].

9.   The blog posts allege that following the Motions hearing, Judge Strickland sent a bailiff to collect [name redacted] from the gallery and had him brought before the bar to where Judge Strickland was standing. Id. [name redacted] further described how Judge Strickland said "Needless to say, I do go on the internet and read about this case... I must say that you have the best website regarding this case." Id.

10.   On April 10, 2010, [name redacted] was interviewed by Miss Anthony's defense team investigator. In that interview, [name

redacted] described how, in February of 2010, he had been hospitalized for a few days. According to [name redacted], he later received a telephone call at home from Judge Strickland, wishing him well. See [name redacted] Affidavit, "Exhibit D" to Motion to Disqualify.

11.   Upon learning, on April 11, 2010, of Judge Strickland's second initiation of contact with a media figure covering Miss Anthony's case, [name redacted], defense counsel prepared the Motion to Disqualify Trial Judge. Said Motion is within the ten days prescribed by law. Florida Rules of Judicial Administration 2.330 (requiring Motion to disqualify to be filed within ten days after **discovery** of **facts** constituting the grounds for the Motion). This recent discovery has precipitated the filing of this Motion. References to the other improprieties give support to the fear of the Defendant in having a fair trial before Judge Strickland.

12.   Judge Strickland's deliberate courting of a well-known media figure raises the inference that Judge Strickland seeks publicity in his own right, and that his rulings and decisions from the bench could be improperly influenced by his desire to secure the outcome that maximizes that publicity.

13.   Due to [name redacted] relentless pro-prosecution bias, as evidenced in his blog posts, any reasonable observer could conclude that Judge Strickland's endorsement of [name redacted] blog is evidence of Judge Strickland's own pro-prosecution slant in this case.

14.   Furthermore, Judge Strickland's telephoning [name redacted] at home, after [name redacted] hospitalization, shows that the courting of [name redacted] in October of 2009 was not a one-

time aberration. To the contrary: Judge Strickland did so after [name redacted] had already publicized the first interaction with the judge in court and that shows that the judge is less interested in maintaining a perception of impartiality than he is in maintaining his contacts among the media, which is a violation of Canon 2 and 3 of the Code of Judicial Conduct.

15.   Judge Strickland's courting favor with media sources violates Canon 2(a) and 3(b) of the Code of Judicial Conduct.

ARGUMENT

The role of an independent judiciary is paramount to American concepts of justice and the rule of law. The American legal system is firmly based upon the principle that an independent, fair and competent judiciary will interpret and apply governing law. Fla. Code Jud. Conduct (2010) (hereafter "Fla. Code"). Judges should aspire at all times to conduct that ensures the greatest possible public confidence in their independence, impartiality, integrity, and competence. ABA Model Code of Jud. Conduct (2007) (hereafter "ABA"). Judges, individually and collectively, must respect and honor the judicial office as a public trust and strive to enhance and maintain confidence in our legal system. Fla. Code. Judges should maintain the dignity of judicial office at all times, and avoid public perception of impropriety in their professional and personal lives. ABA Rule 1.2 cmt. 1 (2007). An independent judiciary requires that judges decide cases according to the law and facts and not according to the views and opinions of outside sources, including that of the public and the media. *See* Fla. Code Canon 3. A judge shall avoid even the appearance of impropriety at all times and whether the conduct would create in reasonable minds a perception that the judge's ability to carry out judicial responsibilities with integrity, impartiality and competence is impaired. ABA Rule 1.2 cmt. 5 (2007). A judge shall disqualify himself or herself where his impartiality might reasonably be questioned. ABA Rule 2.11 (2007). A motion to recuse must be granted if the facts alleged "would prompt a reasonably prudent person to fear that he could not get a fair and impartial trial from the judge," *Nunez v. Backman,* 645 So. 2d 1063, 1064 (Fla. 4th Dist. Ct. App. 1994). In such a circumstance, the facts alleged are to be taken as true and their veracity should not be considered by the judge. *State Farm Mut. Auto. Ins. Co. v. Penland,* 668 So. 2d 200, 204 (Fla. 4th Dist. Ct. App. 1995).

I. Judge Strickland Should Recuse Himself Because His Decisions Show A Bias In Favor Of Media Coverage At The Expense Of Miss Anthony's Constitutional Rights.

Both the Florida and ABA rules of ethical conduct for judges do not merely require the trial judge to show no bias toward either party. Rather, the rules clearly require that the judge avoid creating the public perception of *any* external influence on the judge's behavior and, ultimately, decisions. *See* ABA Rule 2.4 (2007). A judge shall respect and comply with the law and shall act at all times in a manner that promotes public confidence in the integrity and impartiality of the judiciary. Fla. Code Canon 2A. A judge shall not be swayed by partisan interest, public clamor, or fear of criticism. See Fla. Code Canon 3B. This includes any perception that the judge is biased in favor of publicity and media coverage. The unparalleled access of the media in today's world can give rise to the very real fear that a judge might cater to the media and deliver judgments that seek to maximize publicity. *Novartis Pharms. Corp. v. Carnato,* 840 So. 2d 410 (Fla. 4th Dist. Ct. App. 2003) (remanded on other grounds) (Klein, J., dissenting). Even the mere perception that judicial decision making is subject to inappropriate outside influences can severely erode confidence in the Judiciary. ABA Rule 2.4 cmt. 1 (2007).

Miss Anthony will not receive a fair and impartial trial from Judge Strickland because his rulings contemplate media opinion and reaction and are biased in favor of media coverage. Even if a judge's courting of the media covering his case indicates no particular bias toward either party, it can still raise the specter of the judge's interest, intentional or not, in securing the highest level of publicity. The public's faith in the justice system can be equally shaken by a perception that a judge's behavior and decisions are influenced by his desire for media coverage.

Judge Strickland's inappropriate relationship with the media gives rise to a reasonable belief that his rulings are influenced by improper outside sources. This creates an inevitable inference that the media's beliefs, thoughts, and concerns are playing an inappropriate role in his decision-making. A motion to recuse must be granted when a reasonable person would believe that she would not receive a fair decision from a judge who considers media opinion and reaction during a case. *See Coleman v. State,* 866 So. 2d 209.

II. Judge Strickland's Contacts With [name redacted] Inescapably Leads Reasonable People To Conclude That He Is Biased In Favor of Publicity-Enhancing Outcomes.

Judge Strickland's deliberate courting of [name redacted] gives rise to just such an inference of bias. His conduct therefore fatally undermines Miss Anthony's interest in receiving a fair trial. First, a reasonable person could conclude from Judge Strickland's conduct that he has been attempting to court a friendly voice in the blogosphere and to secure positive commentary on his handling of this controversial case. Second, [name redacted] subsequent glowing treatment of Judge Strickland following the judge's solicitation of his goodwill could reasonably raise an inference that Judge Strickland has an interest in maintaining his standing in [name redacted], and by extension, the public's, eyes. The actions by the judge validating and expressing approval of [name redacted] articles calling for the Defendant to die and proclaiming her guilty as charged, as set forth in Exhibits A, B, and C of the Motion, are likely unprecedented in responding to public clamor for conviction and execution of Miss Anthony, long before having a trial.

A. Judge Strickland's deliberate solicitation of [name redacted] raises the reasonable inference that his performance of his judicial duties is compromised by his desire for publicity.

This case is remarkable for the media attention it has attracted ever since Miss Anthony's initial arrest in July 2008. All the major media outlets in the Orlando area have web pages devoted solely to Miss Anthony. [1] Dozens of blogs have forums established exclusively to dissect and analyze Miss Anthony's legal proceedings. [2] One network has hired an in-house attorney for the sole purpose of analyzing the legal issues of Miss Anthony's pre-trial proceedings. [3] Many of these web sites provide lively discussion boards where posters discuss and dissect every aspect of Miss Anthony's court appearances, from Miss Anthony's clothes[4] to the behavior of counsel[5] to the rulings and demeanor of the judge.[6]

As the judge in this case, Judge Strickland must be aware of the intense media scrutiny surrounding Miss Anthony and her upcoming murder trial. Prudent adherence to Florida's Code of Judicial Conduct should have led Judge Strickland to refrain from any contact with the bloggers who follow the case on a day-by-day basis and provide written commentary on nearly every aspect of what transpires in his courtroom. "A judge shall not initiate, permit, or consider ex parte communications, or consider other communications made to the judge outside the presence of the parties concerning a pending or impending proceeding." Fla. Code Jud. Conduct Canon 3(B)(7). Moreover, Florida courts have held that a judge's communications with the media can lead a reasonable person to believe that the judge's impartiality has been compromised. *Coleman v. State,* 866 So. 2d 209, 211 (4 DCA 2004).

In *Novartis Pharms. Corp. v. Carnato,* 840 So. 2d 410 (Fla. 4th Dist. Ct. App. 2003), the defendant sought a writ of prohibition to disqualify the trial judge based on the judge's comments to the media. *Id.* Although the Court of Appeal did not decide the merits of the motion, reversing the trial court's dismissal on procedural grounds and remanding, one judge would have reached the merits to hold that the judge's comments required recusal. *Id.* at 411. Judge Klein's opinion quotes the Court of Appeals for the District of Columbia Circuit to the effect that "[m]embers of the public may reasonably question whether the District Judge's desire for press coverage influenced his judgments, indeed whether a publicity-seeking judge might consciously or subconsciously seek the publicity-maximizing outcome." *Id.* (quoting *United States v. Microsoft Corp.,* 253 F.3d 34, 115 (D.C. Cir. 2001)). The danger that a judge's decisions, rulings, or behavior on the bench might be influenced by a conscious or even subconscious desire for publicity and positive press coverage should function as a constraint on his interactions with the media.

Here, Judge Strickland's purposeful and repeated courting of [name redacted] indicate that he has not followed those constraints. [name redacted] is a prominent blogger covering Miss Anthony's case. His page carries near-daily updates of all the minutiae involved in Miss Anthony's court appearances and the various publicity-seeking characters who have attached themselves to this case. [name redacted] blog post describing his first encounter with Judge Strickland is instructive. First, Judge Strickland sent a court employee, the bailiff, to collect [name redacted] from the gallery and bring him to the judge's exit door. According to [name redacted] Judge Strickland said, "Needless to say, I do go on the Internet and read about this case." *Id.* The judge then further said, "I must say that you have the best web site regarding this case." *Id.*

Taken together, these comments indicate that Judge Strickland a) follows the intensive and non-stop media coverage of Miss Anthony's case, and b) has weighed the relative merits of the various blogs and websites to come to the conclusion that [name redacted] website is "the best." This communication on its own would lead a reasonable person to infer that Judge Strickland has an interest in courting positive media coverage from a friendly source. For him to have taken the extraordinary measure of calling [name redacted] over to the bench in order to solicit his goodwill could lead a reasonable observer to conclude that Judge Strickland may, even subconsciously, be performing his duties in a manner calculated to maximize the publicity and favorable coverage of his handling of this difficult and controversial case. Like the defendant in Coleman, Miss Anthony thus reasonably has "a fear that [s]he could not receive a fair decision from a judge who considers media opinion and reaction during a case." 866 So. 2d at 210.

Judge Strickland's second contact with [name redacted] only strengthens the inference of media bias and Miss Anthony's concurrent fear of not receiving a fair trial. Judge Strickland should have known that his contact with a prominent blogger, focusing nearly exclusively on Miss Anthony's case, could create the impression that his judicial conduct is influenced by his desire for positive coverage. Moreover, [name redacted] responded to Judge Strickland's solicitation by posting a long blog post describing the encounter, positively gushing about his having been selected from all the media figures present for special treatment. In spite of the long post, and the commentary that [name redacted] perceived special relationship with the judge inspired on the blog, Judge Strickland continued the relationship when he telephoned [name redacted] at home in mid-February 2010. [name redacted] did not post his home telephone number on his blog on February 16, 2010. It is unknown how Judge Strickland learned the number. Although of course Judge Strickland's concern for [name redacted] health is commendable, the Florida Judicial Ethics Committee has recently issued an ethics opinion treating the issue of judge-attorney friendships. The Committee warned that "a judge must expect to be the subject of constant public scrutiny, and the impressions that arise from such a relationship." Florida Judicial Ethics Committee, Opinion 2009-20. Here, Judge Strickland's continuing of the relationship—even if purely personal—with a prominent blogger further erodes a reasonable person's belief in his ability to rule from the bench without regard for media reaction.

B. [name redacted] subsequent treatment of Judge Strickland raises the reasonable inference that his performance of his judicial duties is compromised by his desire to maintain the good opinion of the media.

Judge Strickland's initiation of contact with [name redacted] raises a reasonable inference that he seeks positive media coverage of his conduct in Miss Anthony's trial. [name redacted] subsequent treatment of Judge Strickland on his blog, however, raises another inference: that Judge Strickland has an interest in maintaining the good favor of the press he has cultivated. Based on [name redacted] glowing descriptions of Judge Strickland in the months since the October 19, 2009 encounter, an observer could reasonably conclude that Judge Strickland has an interest in maintaining that positive coverage. Miss Anthony thus has a reasonable fear that Judge Strickland's rulings may reflect his desire to sustain his positive reputation in the press and on the blogs, and not his impartial, considered judgment.

After the October 16, 2009 conversation between [name redacted] and Judge Strickland, [name redacted] blog posts increased the number of times he mentioned Judge Strickland. Not only did he increase the number of times he talked about Judge Strickland, he became fervent in his enthusiasm for the judge's performance in the courtroom. On October 27, 2009, a mere nine days after his conversation with Judge Strickland, he wrote a posting titled "They could never ask for a better judge". In this post, he writes how about watching Judge Strickland in the courtroom and how he found "his candor quite refreshing and I welcomed his open-mindedness. I saw live how sharp and focused he remains at all times. He is very well-mannered, well-informed, highly intelligent and because of his personality, humble to boot." [name redacted], "They could never ask for a better judge," [name redacted], October 27, 2009, *available at* http:// [name redacted] wordpress.com/2009/10/27/ they-could-never-ask-for-a-better-judge/. He then attached a supplement from criminal defense lawyers writing positive mentions about Strickland. *Id.*

His subsequent blog entries continue stating zealous pro-Strickland statements, rhapsodizing about Judge Strickland with comments such as "this man is all about integrity and fairness" and "instead of letting each side argue this motion, he patiently waited until the right moment to gracefully interject. That's what I really, really like about him." [name redacted], "A lot of good lawyering today," [name redacted], December 11, 2009, *available at* http://[name redacted].wordpress.com/2009/12/11/a-lot-of-good-lawyering-today/. He also describes how Judge Strickland made wise decisions when he "denied a motion to dismiss double jeopardy charges of check fraud, he denied a motion to stop the Orange County Jail from videotaping meetings with her attorneys and he denied the defense's request to destroy video of any and all visits from her family." [name redacted], "Motion Sickness," [name redacted], December 18, 2009, *available at* http:// [name redacted] wordpress.com/2009/12/18/motion-sickness/. [name redacted] later showed ardent admiration of how "Judge Strickland is not a TV crime solving judge although I'm sure he could get his own show when the trial is over." [name redacted], "Dear Concerned Citizen," [name redacted], January 16, 2010, *available at* [name redacted] wordpress.com/2010/01/16/dear-concerned-citizen/.[name redacted] also opined that "Judge Stan Strickland rules!" and "he is the best judge around." [name redacted], "A Personal Reflection," [name redacted], January 25, 2010, *available at* http:// [name redacted].wordpress.com/2010/01/25/a-personal-reflection/. He later opined, "Judge Strickland will have a lot to say on this matter and we all how know safe, sane and reasonable he is." [name redacted], "Casey Anthony, Guilty of Indigence?", [name redacted], March 6, 2010, *available at* http:// [name redacted].wordpress.com/2010/03/06/casey-guilty-of-indigence/. Only a few weeks later, he described how he notices how Judge Strickland's "relaxed demeanor translates well in court and that he may be larger than life in the scheme of this case he sits in judgment of, but he is far from intimidating. Everyone likes and respects him. He is approachable." [name redacted], "Will Mason Jar the State?", [name redacted], March 19, 2010, *available at* http:// [name redacted].wordpress.com/2010/03/19/will-mason-jar-the-state/. These enthusiastic blog entries after the October 16, 2009 conversation shows how [name redacted] is keeping Judge Strickland in the press in a positive manner.

A reasonable observer, then, could easily infer from Judge Strickland's solicitation of [name redacted] good will and the resulting dramatic increase in positive coverage of Judge Strickland on [name redacted] blog that the judge has a publicity interest in maintaining that coverage. Judge Strickland has admitted that he follows the blogs covering Miss Anthony's case and [name redacted] blog in particular. He also initiated the contact with [name redacted], a prominent blogger whose coverage of Miss Anthony's case has garnered him an award for "Central Florida's Best News Blog." *See* [name redacted], "Orlando's Rockin' Blogs," [name redacted], December 19, 2009, *available at* http://[name redacted].wordpress.com/2009/12/19/orlandos-rockin-blogs-the-orlando-sentinel-orbbies-winners/. A reasonable observer could thus conclude that Judge Strickland has an interest in slanting his conduct on the bench in favor of a publicity-maximizing outcome. *See Novartis Pharms. Corp. v. Carnato,* 840 So. 2d at 411.

III. Judge Strickland's Endorsement of [name redacted] Pro-Prosecution Blog Gives Rise To A Reasonable Inference That Judge Strickland Is Biased Toward The State.

As argued above, Judge Strickland's interactions with [name redacted] give rise to a reasonable inference that he has an interest in both creating and sustaining positive media coverage of his role in the case. That interest, or publicity bias, is unrelated to Judge Strickland's treatment of either party in and of itself; instead, it merely creates a reasonable fear in Miss Anthony that the judge's rulings are affected by his perceptions of the media reaction and opinion. However, Judge Strickland's solicitation and maintenance of his relationship with [name redacted] also raises another, and more sinister, inference: that Judge Strickland's interactions with [name redacted] reflect or could be perceived to reflect a pro-prosecution bias. The tenor of [name redacted] coverage of Miss Anthony's case displays a strong pro-prosecution slant on his part, repeatedly offering his opinion as to Miss Anthony's guilt and nefarious character. Judge Strickland's public courting of [name redacted] could reasonably be seen as an endorsement of those opinions. [name redacted] has written extensively about the Anthony case. His writings are posted to his blog and accessed by Judge Strickland through the Internet. [name redacted] prior writings, of which Judge Strickland feels are "really fair" and the "best blog out there," have titles which include "Casey Anthony must die!," "Caylee's murder: premeditated and pretty stupid too," and "Guilty as CHARGED." The contents of these blog posts—prior to October of 2009, when Judge Strickland first approached [name redacted] predominately include pro-prosecution assertions. In [name redacted] blog posting on February 1, 2009 he gives a synopsis of his theory of the case in which he paints Casey Anthony as a lazy, foul-mouthed liar who killed her child and was too stupid to realize that the body would be found when she disposed of it so close to the Anthony home. [name redacted] theory paints Ms. Anthony as just another dumb party girl willing to do anything to maintain her dumb party girl image. He asserts his belief that Caylee's death was the result of a premeditated crime and that murdering Caylee was the way for Ms. Anthony to return to her carefree days of her childhood. [name redacted] goes as far as to assert that Ms. Anthony was a psychopath with low self-esteem who sometimes has a violent side and whose impulsive nature is what led her to kill Caylee. The blog entry concludes by asserting that Ms. Anthony is another murderer who deserves punishment and that when she does, Ms. Anthony will become a footnote in history. *See* [name redacted] "Caylee's murder: premeditated and pretty stupid, too," [name redacted], February 1, 2009, *available at* http:// [name redacted].wordpress.com/2009/ 02/01/caylees-murder-premeditated-and-pretty-stupid-too/. These are the very assertions to which Judge Strickland was presumably referring when he concluded that [name redacted] has "the best blog going out there," one that is "really fair."

[name redacted] pro-prosecution bias is not limited to his antipathy for Miss Anthony. His blog has also repeatedly attacked the members of Miss

Anthony's defense team. In one blog posting, he accused a member of the defense team of being a liar and that a Bar Grievance Committee's finding "insufficient evidence" against the lawyer as "impossible". [name redacted], "Baez beats bar," [name redacted], September 1, 2009, *available at* http://[name redacted].wordpress.com). In another posting, [name redacted] refers to another member of the defense team joining the case as "someone new to hate." [name redacted], "Hearing Updates," [name redacted], May 28, 2009, *available at* http://[nameredacted] wordpress.com/2009/05/28/andrea-d-ly-on-caseys-new-death-penalty-qualified-attorney/). These posts indicate that the blogger so assiduously courted by Judge Strickland harbored not only a bias against Miss Anthony but, by extension, against the members of her defense team—and that Judge Strickland, who apparently had been reading [name redacted] blog for some time before the October 19, 2009 encounter, knew or should have known of that bias. A judge must perform judicial duties impartially and fairly. A judge who manifests bias on any basis in a proceeding impairs the fairness of the proceeding and brings the judiciary into disrepute. Clearly, Judge Strickland's perception of this case is pro-prosecution. His bias is evident by his assertion that [name redacted] has a "fair" account of the facts in this case. A judge shall disqualify himself where his impartiality might reasonably be questioned. Fla. Code Jud. Conduct, Canon 3(E)(1). In this case, Judge Strickland should be disqualified. His bias impairs the fairness of the proceedings in this case and violates Ms. Anthony's rights.

When a Motion to disqualify is filed, the judge is required to immediately rule on the Motion. Shah v. Harding, 839 So.2d 765 (3 DCA 2003). In ruling on the Motion, the judge shall determine only the legal sufficiency of the Motion and shall not pass on the truth of the facts alleged. Knarick v. State, 866 So.2d 165 (2 DCA 2004). The Court must view the alleged facts from the perspective of the moving party, Frengel v. Frengel, 880 So.2d 763 (2 DCA 2004), and not the Court's own perception of his ability to act fairly and impartially. Valdes-Fauli v. Valdes-Fauli, 903 So.2d 214 (3 DCA 2005). It is a feeling that resides in the movant's mind, not a question of how the judge feels. Wargo v. Wargo, 669 So.2d 1123 (4 DCA 1996).

CONCLUSION

Judge Strickland's duty to preside over this case with impartiality is of utmost importance. His repeated and deliberate courting of a prominent media figure in this case has undermined the appearance of impartiality to the degree that Miss Anthony has a reasonable fear that she may not receive a fair trial. Because Judge Strickland's actions and comments have raised the inference of judicial bias, this Court should grant Miss Anthony's Motion to Disqualify Trial Judge.

Respectfully submitted,

J. CHENEY MASON,

one of the attorneys for CASEY MARIE ANTHONY

---

[1] See, e.g., The Orlando Sentinel, http://www.orlandosentinel.com/news/local/cayleeanthony/; WFTV-9, http://www.wftv.com/caseyanthony/index.html; WESH-2, http://www.wesh.com/caseyanthony/index.html; WOFL-35, http://www.myfoxorlando.com/subindex/news/ anthony_case; Central News Florida 13, http://www.cfnews13.com/Features/CaseyAnthony/ Default.aspx.

[2] See, e.g., "The Caylee Daily," available at www.cayleedaily.com; "Caylee Anthony," available at www.cayleeanthony.wordpress.com.

[3] See William J. Sheaffer, "Breaking My First Blog," WFTV-9, November 10, 2009, available at http://www.wftv.com/caseyanthonyblog/index.html.

[4] See, e.g., "Scared Monkeys" comment thread, March 12, 2009, available at http://scared-monkeys.net/index.php?topic=4660.265;wap2.

[5] See, e.g., Topix.com comment thread, April 5, 2010, available at http://www.topix.com/forum/source/wtvr/TIFF7FN76U1O75SOD.

[6] See, e.g., Orlandosentinel.com comment thread, January 25, 2010, available at http://blogs.orlandosentinel.com/entertainment_tv_tvblog/2010/01/casey-anthony-wkmg-studiesjudge-stan-stricklands-sentencing-record-hints-at-whats-ahead-today.html.

The Rules of Judicial Administration state that when a legally sufficient Motion to Disqualify is filed, a judge must sign an order disqualifying him or herself. The judge is not allowed to do anything in such a case, other than make the determination of the legal sufficiency of the motion based upon the standard of whether or not a reasonable person would fear an inability to have a fair trial before this judge. It is fundamental that if the judge objects to a legally sufficient motion, or takes issue with any facts alleged in it, the mere fact of him doing so establishes a conflict and subsequent basis for recusal, which is then automatically carried out. Furthermore, if the judge refuses to rule on the motion for a period of thirty days, then it is deemed granted, and the judge is removed from the case.

In keeping with the behavior that had resulted in the necessity to file this motion in the first place, Judge Strickland was not content simply to acknowledge the legal sufficiency of the motion, but accompanied his acknowledgement with a several-page response, written apparently for personal reasons. In the end, however, he had no choice but to recuse himself from the case.

The prosecution team, as it turned out, were very happy with this development. I learned that they had been afraid that Judge Strickland might not impose the death penalty. Nobody knew who our next judge would be, as it was up to the chief judge to reassign the case; but the prosecution was hopeful.

"You might be sorry," prosecutor Ashton quipped. "You might get somebody worse than Judge Strickland. You might get Judge Perry."

7

Hallucinogenic Forensics

We might generally define science as a body of knowledge covering certain general truths as obtained and tested via a consistent scientific methodology. Forensic science is that branch of science that is deemed suitable for use in courts of law or reliable public discussion. Junk science, forensic or otherwise, is simply speculative: it comprises those claims, theories and procedures that, though scientific in appearance, are not verifiable under any consistent methodology.

Upon a request from Congress in 2009, the National Research Council of the National Academy of Sciences—an institution established in 1863 by President Lincoln—published "Strengthening Forensic Science in the United States: A Path Forward." The goal of this publication was to set forth the need for standards in forensic science, and address some of the obstacles to such standards. "If evidence and laboratory tests are mishandled or improperly analyzed," the paper stated, "the scientific evidence carries a false sense of significance; or if there is bias, incompetence or a lack of adequate internal controls for the evidence introduced by the forensic scientists and their laboratories, the jury or Court can be misled and this could lead to a wrongful conviction or exoneration. If juries lose confidence in the reliability of forensic testimony valid evidence might be discounted and some innocent persons might be convicted or guilty individuals acquitted."

Concerns for such miscarriages of justice should weigh much more heavily than they do on the minds of American citizens. Television and other forms of popular entertainment too often give us the illusion that the science of forensics is objective and not subject to human error, mistake or bias. Jurors, accordingly, are far more easily swayed by the testimony of persons bearing the title of "expert witnesses," whose opinions are presumed to represent fact. Unfortunately, this is far from the truth. Research, especially in recent years, has shown us that many of the even established claims and methodologies of scientific forensics are often simply wrong. This is critical to an understanding of justice and an effort to avoid obstructing it.

Again in 2009, the Virginia Law Review published a study of the many cases in which a defendant had been wrongfully convicted and later found to be innocent. They found that all of these cases had involved prosecution "experts," a majority of whom had presented evidence that was misstated or invalid. This travesty was not just a matter of one or two experts; the study analyzed 72 experts in 137 cases. Some of these "experts" had misrepresented their background and training in order to be admitted into the trial. Many had misrepresented the facts upon which their conclusions were based, leaving out or minimizing important information. Disturbingly, the study noted, "in the few cases in which invalid forensic science was challenged, judges seldom provided relief."

Some of these faulty experts are honestly mistaken—not only in the facts, but in the motives underlying their pursuit of them. People have an innate desire to please, and if an expert is hired by one side of a case, it is natural enough that he or she might subconsciously want to help the side that's paying the bills. Furthermore, people cannot help bringing their own personal biases to a case. If an expert believes a defendant is guilty prior to conducting his or her research, the research may very well not be as rigorously balanced as in a case in which he or she knows nothing about the case at all. This kind of bias, in which we find what we have decided beforehand that we want to find, happens so frequently that there is a shorthand term for it; it's called confirmation bias.

The Chief Medical Examiner in the "Case Against Casey" was, like so many others, keenly and actively aware of the news reports surrounding the case prior to her involvement in it. When Caylee's remains were found, she was on a trip out of town; and so keen was her interest that she canceled her trip, catching the first plane back to Orlando so she could take over the investigation immediately—even though an Assistant Medical Examiner, fully competent and experienced, was already on the job. What she and the case's other forensic examiners would eventually conclude might have been predicted, like the bias of Judge Strickland, from the level of their exposure to the news; though as in Judge Strickland's case, the specifics would prove rather shocking.

The trial of Casey Anthony involved some of the most complicated forensic claims ever put forth in a criminal case. We saw almost everything, with the exception of blood-spatter evidence and ballistics, including some scientific claims that had never been seen anywhere before.

Recall that the State, as in other prosecution cases, had no shortage of experts and no restriction on its funding. One might assume that this circumstance would heighten the quality of the science conducted on behalf of the prosecution; but in this case, interestingly enough, it proved a major cause for the prevalence of junk science on that side. Money and prestige contribute just as readily, and perhaps more so, to slipshod work as they do to excellence and with these motivations running counter to their scientific integrity, a number of the prosecution's "experts" were more than willing to bend the truth. The underfunded defense, on the contrary, had to rely, in its investigation of these claims, on volunteer scientists—those whose interest in the truth was strong enough to justify their working for little or no money, and at the risk of significant social and professional ostracism.

It would be extremely difficult for a single volume to cover all of the areas of real and alleged forensic science that were touched upon in this case, I have elected to discuss some of the major points here, grouped into five separate areas of forensic evidence: the alleged odor in the trunk of Cindy Anthony's car; the hair found there; the alert given by a sniffing dog at the Anthonys' home; the Anthonys' neighbor's shovel; the duct tape and heart-shaped sticker found with Caylee's body; and other details pertaining to the site where her body was found.

One of the quotes most often replayed in the media surrounding the case was the original 911 call from Cindy Anthony, in which she claimed that her daughter's car smelled like it had "had a damn dead body in it." When law enforcement officers and their partners, the media, learned that Caylee Anthony had been missing for some thirty days, the grandmother's hysterical proclamation became the proverbial shot heard around the world. There was no calling it back, even with a jury acquittal.

This incident had occurred one day in the summer of 2008, when George and Cindy "happened to notice" a paper of some kind affixed to the front door of their home. This, as it turned out, was a notice advising them that their car had been impounded, and that if they wanted to get it back, they would have to pay the towing and storage fee. Cindy and George had thought their daughter Casey had been in possession of the car, as it was really hers as far as family use was concerned.

After taking off from work, Cindy met George, they collected the 400–plus dollars they needed to pay the charges, and George went to retrieve the car. It should be noted that nobody near where the car had been left for several days had mentioned anything about any conspicuous odor, nor had the man who had initially towed the car.

When George Anthony went to pick up the car, however, he noticed an unusual smell. When he opened the trunk of the car, he found its cause: a bag of garbage—household garbage, evidently, with rotted contents inside. The tow-truck driver simply lifted this bag out of the truck and threw it over the fence of his property into an area by a dumpster, and George drove the car home to Hopespring Drive. At this point one can legitimately wonder if, as alleged, there had been the distinct and disgusting odor of human decomposition in the car, how George was able to drive home without noticing it.

During the many media descriptions of this issue and the claims to unique personal experience made by its talking-head detectives, one phrase was frequently repeated: "Once you've smelled a dead body you never forget it." Now this, it is worth pointing out, is a perfect example of the kind of claim made in support of what I am calling hallucinogenic forensics. It's like a schoolyard rumor: one person says it, another likes the way it sounds and repeats it, and soon it's being repeated all over the place. After hearing and repeating the claim enough times, people begin to attribute an aura of factuality to it. Scientifically speaking, there are so many things wrong with this claim, and others like it, that legitimate scientists and medical examiners could spend hours discoursing on the topic. A forensic scientist and criminologist of world renown, Dr. Henry Lee, was initially involved with the defense team on this case. Dr. Lee informed me that all such claims to consistency in the odor of corpses, such that "once you smell it, you never forget it," were patently absurd. There are, he affirmed, numerous variables that affect the smell of corpses and make such a claim hallucinogenic; including, but not limited to, the age of the corpse; its race; its size; its nationality and resulting dietary histories; the location it was found; the length of time it had spent in that location; its exposure to the elements, and what those elements were; and the nature of its death. While, therefore, there may be some similarities in odor between corpses in different cases, it's a long way from being a generally applicable forensic fact.

Why had Cindy made this allegation in her original 911 call? The prosecution tried to justify her impression with the fact that she was a nurse and worked at a hospital; yet the fallacy of this argument is quickly exposed. While it may be true that people die in hospitals, hospitals don't keep bodies lying around decomposing so as to allow even the workers there to experience the odor referred to. What can her claim have proven, then, beyond the suggestiveness of her own—and, subsequently, others'—imagination?

When the police responding to Cindy's call arrived at the Anthonys' home, the car, of course, was there. It is important to note that the law enforcement officers who came, even having been prepared beforehand via Cindy's hysterical call, did not smell or claim to smell anything. The responding deputy and sergeant supervisor would later acknowledge, under oath, that they had not smelled anything, as would the deputy dispatched for the specific purpose of seizing the car and taking it to the CSI laboratory of the Orange County Sheriff's Department. These are undisputed facts; they are the testimonies given in the trial, as well as in pre-trial depositions. It might also be remembered that in trial Cindy would claim that she had made up her observation to get the cops' attention in response to her call. Yet due to the contagious nature of that observation, and of the sound-bite pseudoscience elicited in support of it, this was one of the most widely influential parts of the prosecution's argument.

Once the car was taken to the CSI lab, a forensic examination of it was begun. One of the detectives in charge had apparently read a magazine article about Arpad Vass, Ph.D., a scientist with the Oakridge National Laboratory in Knoxville, Tennessee. Dr. Vass had previously been involved with what is known as the "Body Farm," an ongoing project in connection with the University of Tennessee in which studies are conducted upon the decomposition of human bodies.

In general, the process at the Body Farm involves placing donated bodies at various depths of burial, with some left aboveground, and studying what happens to them over varying lengths of time and under varying circumstances. In some cases, pipes are inserted into the corpses so that decomposition gases can be collected and scientifically examined. This project has been going on for some years, but has never resulted in any scientifically reliable information. Initially, Dr. Vass and his team claimed to have identified various chemical compositions contained in the trapped and examined gases; but this number has varied as the project has gone on, from as few as 32 to more than 470. When Dr. Vass was asked if there is a single chemical composition, or combination of chemical compounds, unique to the decomposition of a human body, he had to admit that there is not.

Nevertheless, the prosecution, in their "Case Against Casey," insisted on relying heavily on conjectures derived from this rather shaky science. The CSI detective in charge of the investigation of the car contacted Dr. Vass, who instructed him to contact a local expert in forensic chemistry from the University of Central Florida, Dr. Michael Sigman, and with his aid, to trap some of the air from the trunk of the car for analysis.

Dr. Michael Sigman—who certainly had and has expert credentials and qualifications—extracted and trapped two samples of air from the car. One sample was sent to Dr. Vass's people at the Oakridge National Laboratory, and the other went with Dr. Sigman to the UCF lab. While the Vass team claimed that their testing revealed an "extremely high" level of chloroform, Dr. Sigman's very similar test revealed that the substance most substantially detectable in the sample was gasoline. Similarly, when forensic scientists sent out samples of the trunk carpet for testing, the people at the Oakridge National Laboratory claimed that these samples showed very high levels of chloroform, whereas similar testing done by the Federal Bureau of Investigation revealed that the chloroform levels were "very, very low."

Now, why was everyone talking about chloroform to begin with? It was simply because the initial air-sample testing, conducted with a gas chromatograph-mass spectrometer, had revealed a spike in its analytical graph, and Dr. Vass had hastened to point out that chloroform, the chemical detected thereby, is one of the chemical substances commonly found in decomposition. Later the prosecution would bring in a sensational new theory, that chloroform had actually been used to poison Caylee; but at this stage, it was enough simply to prove its presence. Never mind the fact that nobody else had claimed to smell anything out of the ordinary in the trunk of the car; never mind the fact that chloroform is only one of the myriad of chemical compounds found in decomposition, and is also found in the air surrounding much commoner areas, like swimming pools; the prosecution had its lead, and they were determined to follow it.

In line with this pursuit, the Oakridge National Laboratory made arrangements to purchase a car similar to the Anthony car in make, model, and year from a junkyard in Knoxville, Tennessee. They then cut out samples of the trunk's carpet and tested them for the presence of chloroform, as had been found in the subject car. This testing found, clearly and unequivocally, that the chloroform readings in this car were identical to those in the Anthony car.

Doubting the odds of a junkyard car in Tennessee having had, at some point in time, a decaying and decomposing body in its trunk, the defense team then went to Knoxville to take the deposition testimonies of Dr. Vass and the other scientists related to this investigation. We learned that there was no confirmed "chain of custody" concerning where the various carpet samples had been; apparently they had been placed in different cans and left on Dr. Vass's desk. This disrespect for the sanctity of trial evidence was shocking, but more so was Dr. Vass's admission that he and his scientists had not followed any established testing protocol. Nor were these the only evidences of Dr. Vass's loose science. At another time, working on the same hypothetical principles, he had worked with others to develop a metal detector–like machine for finding buried bodies, which they had called the "Labrador." They had brought the Labrador to the ranch where Charles Manson had allegedly buried his victims, and immediately it had registered a "hit." Certain they would find a body to corroborate the value of their machine, Vass and his team dug, and dug, and dug—and never found a single body.

This was the kind of speculative science that had gained such renown among the prosecutors? This sort of testimony was being admitted into the trial for a woman's life?

In addition to the alleged odor in the trunk of Cindy Anthony's car—regarding which nobody could seem to agree—CSI technicians found a hair there.

The hair was described as being "similar" to one they believed could have been from the missing child. Of course, it could have come from Casey; it could have come from Cindy; it could have come from anybody, at any time. Later, the car—which had been continuously in the sheriff's keeping—was examined by criminologist Henry Lee, who, without much difficulty, found sixteen additional hairs there. The question was, what significance did this hair have to the case at hand?

Contrary to popular belief, there is no specific way to positively identify a hair as having been shed by a particular person, or in a particular set of circumstances, yet many people have been wrongfully convicted on such unsubstantiated assumptions. In many of these cases, the scientists that talk about similarities in hair will simply opine that a found hair is "consistent with" one from a crime scene or a particular subject, and imagination does the rest. So what was the meaning of the hair to the prosecution in this case?

There's a new field of forensic "science" being explored called hair banding. The basic theory underlying this science is that when a human hair is connected to a deceased and decomposing body, near the follicle end of the hair there will appear a dark, ring-like band encircling it. Interestingly, the hair first found allegedly had this "banding" around it; none of the rest did. The State claimed that this single hair was proof that a decomposing body had been in the trunk, and that it must have been that of little Caylee.

Now, this testimony was being offered to the jury as evidence that the hair had come from a dead body, rather than having been shed naturally from a live one. Interestingly, the prosecution's experts confirmed that we humans lose between fifty and two hundred hairs per day, meaning that one person could lose 73,000 hairs in a single year. When these hairs fall out, they naturally decompose; so the critical question for the experts was, how does a hair decompose when it's shed from a dead body, versus how it decomposes when it's shed from a live body?

It turns out that there's not a great deal of difference—and that what difference there is, is established only on very uncertain grounds. The State's expert acknowledged that there were no published standards on how to evaluate hair for hair banding; no standard number of micrometers from the root to the alleged band; no standard band width; and no standard band color. More importantly, there has never been a confirmed case of hair banding having been established from a single hair.

Furthermore, she acknowledged under oath that, though the training to qualify one as an "expert" in post-mortem hair banding only occupied a six-month period, she herself was not such an expert, and had simply had informal experience with the phenomenon. She had never previously been allowed to testify in court as an expert on the subject matter of post-mortem hair banding or decomposition, nor had she ever testified that one hair with apparent decomposition had definitely come from a dead body. This was the first case in which she had ever made claims of the sort she was making for her fledgling "science"—claims upon which the prosecution was, nevertheless, ready to argue a capital verdict.

We have all seen numerous dramatic productions purporting to show the great efforts made, and results achieved, by dogs in various forensic capacities. Some are trained to find drugs; some, water or termites; some, dead bodies. The number of convictions, and wrongful convictions, hinging on such "dog sniffs" is mind-boggling, and more than a little disturbing, given the incidence of error associated with this practice.

Several years ago there was a case in Brevard County, Florida, in which a young man was wrongfully convicted of violently raping a woman. The detectives in that case used a dog that they claimed could trace the odor of a person even months or years later, and over water! Unfortunately, on the insistence of the judge, the jury bought this story, and the defendant was convicted.

Twenty-four years later, I was part of the Innocence Project team that was finally able to get the hardheaded prosecution to agree to a modern DNA test of various pieces of forensic evidence taken from that crime scene, which test absolutely excluded the defendant from having been the contributor. He was then freed from the wrongful conviction, and later the Florida Legislature paid him $2.1 million. One would think that the notoriety of this wrong conviction, based largely on faulty dog-sniff evidence, would have given pause for thought to Casey Anthony's prosecution and kept them from hinging their case so confidently on dog-sniff evidence of their own; but sadly, not so.

In this case, a dog was brought up to search the Anthony residence and their little backyard, whereupon the dog "alerted"—signaling to the police that there was a body buried in the backyard. A second dog was then brought in for confirmation, but contrary to the hopes of the prosecution, this dog did not alert. Furthermore, in a subsequent search, nothing was found—not a drop of blood, not a fingernail, not a body, nothing. Yet the first dog's "evidence" was admitted and broadcast in the news, fueling a great deal of rabid speculation.

This evidence was challenged vigorously in pretrial motions. The handler was exposed as having testified differently about what did or did not happen with the dog. A test of the dog was conducted to see whether it would alert on the subject vehicle at the crime-scene lab; during which test some experts said there were two cars, and the dog only alerted on one, while others said there was only one car. We tried to prevent the admission of dog-sniff evidence altogether because of its lack of scientific standards and records as to how many times such dogs have been wrong.

The Supreme Court of Florida, in a ruling that seemed favorable to our side, agreed that such evidence could not be admitted unless the prosecution complied with certain requirements, including producing logs confirming the training of the dog in question, which would include its error rates. This opinion came out near the middle of our trial; and accordingly, we attempted to get Judge Perry, the trial judge brought in to replace Stan Strickland, to strike and/or prevent the relevant testimony, or otherwise seek a "curative instruction" that would direct the jury to disregard it. The judge, predictably, overruled our objection.

Ironically, he was later vindicated. During the preliminary outlining of this book, the United States Supreme Court reversed the Florida Supreme Court's decision on a few fine points. Now it appears that the door has been opened for forensic dog-sniff evidence to be admitted even from dogs whose handlers have not maintained the appropriate records to prove their efficacy. It seems we will have to rely, at least for the foreseeable future, on the sensibility of our juries to reject the charlatan-like assurances that so often accompany such claims.

During the investigation, one of George and Cindy Anthony's neighbors claimed that during the summer—on July the 16th of 2008 in particular—Casey had come over to his house to borrow a shovel. He claimed that she had said she wanted to borrow the shovel for the purpose of cutting out some unwanted shoots of bamboo growing up in the paved area of the Anthony family's backyard.

When the neighbor related this information to the law enforcement community, they eagerly pursued this new forensic detail. The shovel was bagged—naturally under the ever-watchful eyes of the news media hovering in helicopters overhead—and the FBI took it off to their multimillion-dollar labs and subjected it to every test available.

Now, absolutely nothing related this shovel, in any regard whatsoever, to Caylee's death, or even to Casey. As will be seen later in our discussion of the discovery of the child, there was no evidence that the child had been buried, or that a shovel had been involved in any way with the child's death. Had the child's remains been found buried, one could reasonably argue that the shovel could be relevant; but since that wasn't the case, the shovel could only function in the trial as a means to prejudice the jury against Casey.

Accordingly, the defense team filed a motion to exclude the testimony regarding this shovel, on the simple grounds that there was no proven scientific link between it and any part of Caylee's death or disappearance, and that it therefore added unduly to the prejudicial bias already prevalent in the case. Under the Rules of Evidence, even if an item or issue *could* be relevant to a trial, when the likelihood of prejudice outweighs whatever probative value may be attributed to the evidence, it is not allowed, and this seemed decidedly such a circumstance.

I reproduce our motion here, as follows.

IN THE CIRCUIT COURT FOR THE NINTH JUDICIAL CIRCUIT
IN AND FOR ORANGE COUNTY, FLORIDA

STATE OF FLORIDA,   CASE NO.: 482008-CF-0015606-O
       Plaintiff,   Judge Perry

vs.

CASEY MARIE ANTHONY,
       Defendant.
_____/

MOTION IN LIMINE REGARDING TESTIMONY OF NEIGHBOR BRIAN BURNER IN REFERENCE TO SHOVEL

COMES NOW THE Defendant, CASEY MARIE ANTHONY, by and through her

attorneys J. CHENEY MASON and JOSE BAEZ and, pursuant to Rules 401 and 403, Florida

Rules of Evidence, and the United States and Florida Constitutions, moves this Court in Limine

to prohibit the introduction into evidence in the trial of this cause of any testimony by one Mr.

Brian Burner, a neighbor of the Defendant's, as it relates to allegations of the Defendant

borrowing a shovel.

The shovel has not been linked by witness or any forensic evidence whatsoever to any aspect

of this case and, accordingly, is irrelevant and immaterial.

MEMORANDUM OF LAW IN SUPPORT OF MOTION IN LIMINE TO PRECLUDE CERTAIN TESTIMONY OF MR. BRIAN BURNER

A motion in limine is used to shorten trial, simplify issues, and reduce the potential for

mistrial, thereby moving the case toward a conclusion on the merits. *Rosa v. Fl. Power & Light

Co.*, 636 So. 2d 60 (Fla. 2d DCA 1994); *See also* § 90.403, Fla. Stat. (2009) ("Relevant evidence

is inadmissible if its probative value is substantially outweighed by the danger of unfair

1

prejudice, confusion of issues, misleading the jury, or needless presentation of cumulative evidence."). Further, "[a] motion in limine ... is generally used to prevent the introduction of improper evidence, the mere mention of which at trial would be prejudicial." *Dailey v. Multicon Development, Inc.*, 417 So. 2d 1106 (Fla. 4th DCA 1982); *Adkins v. Seaboard Coast Line R. Co.*, 351 So. 2d 1088 (Fla. 2d DCA 1977).

Additionally, Florida Statute § 90.105 provides, "[t]he court shall determine preliminary questions concerning the qualification of a person to be a witness, the existence of a privilege, or the admissibility of evidence." Also, § 90.104(2) provides "[i]n cases tried by a jury, a court shall conduct proceedings, to the maximum extent practicable, in such a manner as to prevent inadmissible evidence from being suggested to the jury by any means." Based upon due process, a fair trial, an impartial jury, and effective assistance of counsel, Ms. Anthony is entitled to a hearing and ruling on the following issue before the selection of a jury.

STATEMENT OF THE FACTS

Based on Discovery Materials provided by the State, Mr. Brian Burner engaged in a Taped Interview conducted by Detective Appling Wells on July 17, 2008 (hereinafter Interview 1). Based on the transcript of the interview, Mr. Burner stated that, during the week of June 16, 2008: "...Casey approached me and said that she couldn't find the key to their shed and want (sp.) to know if I had a shovel she could borough (sp.) to dig up...um...a bamboo root that she's been tripping over...and I agree I said yea I have a shovel that you can use." (Interview 1 Tran. P. 3; 21-24). Further, Mr. Burner stated, "I gave her the shovel." (Interview 1, P. 4; 7). Subsequently, two more interviews were conducted, which reiterated this point. (Taped Transcript of Brian Burner Interview Conducted by Corporal Edwards, July 30, 2008; Transcript of Brian Burner Conducted by Det. Appling Wells, August 12, 2008). Mr. Burner also stated that

2

Ms. Anthony returned the shovel that same day. (Interview 1, P. 6;17). Further, he stated that he noticed nothing unusual about the shovel or Ms. Anthony's demeanor. (Interview 1; p. 10, 10-14).

ARGUMENT

Mr. Brian Burner's testimony related to the shovel, as well as any related reference to such testimony, must be precluded from trial in order to protect Ms. Anthony's right to a fair trial. First, the testimony regarding the shovel is utterly irrelevant to the case at hand. Second, any alleged probative value is substantially outweighed by its potential prejudicial effect on the jury.

I.   MR. BURNER'S STATEMENTS THAT MS. ANTHONY BORROWED A SHOVEL FROM HIM ARE UTTERLY IRRELEVANT AND HAVE NO TENDENCY TO PROVE OR DISPROVE A MATERIAL FACT AT ISSUE.

The test of admissibility is relevancy. *Reddish v. State*, 167 So. 2d 858, 861 (Fla. 1964); FLA. STAT. § 90.401 (2009). Relevant evidence is evidence that has "any logical tendency to prove or disprove a fact" in issue. *State v. Taylor*, 648 So. 2d 701, 704 (Fla. 1995). Although evidence tending to prove or disprove one material element of an offense is relevant, whether Ms. Anthony borrowed a shovel is irrelevant and has no tendency to prove or disprove a material fact at issue in this capital criminal prosecution. Specifically, Ms. Anthony has been charged with Capital First Degree Murder, Aggravated Child Abuse, and four counts of Providing False Information to a Law Enforcement Officer. (Indictment). Evidence that Ms. Anthony borrowed a shovel from her neighbor does not tend to prove any element of the offenses for which she is charged and, thus, is inadmissible as irrelevant.

3

Shennett v. State, 937 So. 2d 287 (Fla. 4th DCA 2006) is instructive. In *Shennett*, the

defendant was charged with burglary and possession of burglary tools based on allegations that

he broke into a Dodge Caravan by shattering a window with a spark plug. When the Defendant

was subsequently stopped by Law Enforcement, a search of his vehicle produced a Ziploc baggie

which contained a screwdriver and pieces of porcelain from a spark plug. Evidence of the

screwdriver and the porcelain pieces were admitted at trial and the defendant was convicted on

both burglary and possession of burglary tools. *Id.* On appeal, the Court found that the trial court

had abused its discretion by admitting the screwdriver and the porcelain pieces into evidence.

Specifically, the Court stated:

> The screw driver was irrelevant to the issues at trial because it did not 'tend to
> prove or disprove a material fact' in the case. § 90.401, Fla. Stat. (2005). The
> burglary tool which Schennett was charged with possessing was "porcelain
> pieces." There was no evidence that he used the screwdriver in any way to
> burglarize Brown's minivan. The screwdriver had no connection with either
> charged offense. *See Rigdon v. State*, 621 So. 2d 475, 478 (Fla. 4th DCA 1993).

Id. at 292-93.

Similarly, whether or not Ms. Anthony borrowed a shovel from Mr. Burner does not in

any way make the charged offenses more or less probable. There is no evidence that Ms.

Anthony used or intended to use the borrowed shovel to facilitate the commission of any of the

charged crimes, nor is there any assertion of such. *LaVallee v. State*, 958 So. 2d 509, 511 (Fla. 4th

DCA 2007) (stating where a defendant possessed a screwdriver and gloves shortly after a

burglary and even during a burglary was irrelevant, as there was "simply no connection shown

between appellant's possession of the items and the crime charged"); (Contrast *Rebjebian v.

State*, 44 So. 2d 81 (Fla. 1949) where the defendant was caught in the commission of a burglary,

4

had gained entry to a locked dwelling, and was found to possess a screwdriver while in the dwelling, the screwdriver was admissible).

Further, in an analogous case, the Fifth DCA found that an ineffective assistance of counsel claim had merit where the defendant's attorney failed to object to the admissibility of firearms found in the defendant's home when the firearms were not linked to the charged crime of Attempted First Degree Murder. *Moore v. State*, 1 So. 3d 1177 (Fla. 5th DCA 2009). In coming to this conclusion, the Court stated:

> Of course, if there was no evidence linking any of these firearms to the charged crime, evidence of the firearms would be irrelevant, and should have been excluded upon proper objection. *See, e.g., Sosa v. State*, 639 So. 2d 173 (Fla. 3d DCA 1994) (holding that it was error to admit into evidence .380 cartridges found in the defendant's car where there was no link established between the cartridges and the crime charges); *Huhn v. State*, 511 So. 2d 583 (Fla. 4th DCA 1987) (holding that it was error to admit into evidence a gun purchased by the defendant which was not connected with the charged crimes); *Rigdon v. State*, 621 So. 2d 475 (Fla. 4th DCA 1993) (reversing a conviction for aggravated assault with a firearm where the trial court admitted into evidence a semi-automatic weapon on the defendant's bed because there had been no connection between the weapon and the crime.)

Id. at 1178-79.

Similarly, in the present case, there is no evidence which links the shovel to the commission of the any of the charges. And while the above case cites a string of authority related directly to the inadmissibility of firearms, rather than the shovel at issue in the present case, the proposition still stands that the admission of irrelevant evidence creates a danger that the jury will base a conviction on information that is not related to the charges at hand. *Rosa v. Fl. Power & Light Co.*, 636 So. 2d 60 (Fla. 2d DCA 1994) (stating a motion in limine helps to shorten

5

trials, simplify issues, and reduce the potential for mistrial, thereby moving the case toward a conclusion on the actual merits).

Where a shovel has been mentioned (often fleetingly) in a published opinion as presumably relevant, admissible evidence in a capital first degree premeditated murder trial, the shovel was directly related to the charge. *Twilegar v. State*, 42 So. 3d 177, 186 (Fla. 2010) (mentioned shovel in appeal where a shovel was found at the burial site and the victim had been buried while, likely, still breathing); *Cole v. State*, 36 So. 3d 597, 600 (Fla. 2010) (mentioning shovels where the shovels were used to dig a grave and bury the victims alive); *Rodgers v. State*, 934 So. 2d 1207, 1224 (Fla. 2006) (mentioning a list created by the defendant, one of the items on which was a shovel, where the list was made by the defendant which included items "needed to effectuate the plan"). The present case presents no such scenario, in that the shovel at issue was clearly not used in the commission of any of the charged crimes. As such, admitting the shovel would be in violation of Fla. Stat. § 90.104(2), which requires "[i]n cases tried by a jury, a court shall conduct proceedings, to the maximum extent practicable, in such a manner as to prevent inadmissible evidence from being suggested to the jury by any means."

II. ANY ALLEGED PROBABTIVE VALUE OF MR. BURNER'S STATEMENTS ARE SUBSTAINTIALLY OUTWEIGHED BY THE DANGER OF UNFAIR PREJUDICE TO MS. ANTHONY.

As stated above, the shovel is irrelevant to the charges in the present case. However, if this Honorable Court does deem testimony regarding the shovel somewhat relevant, such testimony must still be excluded. FLA. STAT. § 90.403 (2009) (Relevant evidence is inadmissible if its probative value is substantially outweighed by the danger of unfair prejudice, confusion of the issues, misleading the jury or needless presentation of cumulative evidence). In *Huhn v. State*,

6

511 So. 2d 583, 588 (Fla. 4th DCA 1987), the Court found that evidence related to the purchase of a firearm was unfairly prejudicial, where the firearm was not linked to the commission of the charged offense. The Court stated "evidence concerning the gun and the AFT records of his purchase of this and other guns was inadmissible. He says that because the particular gun was not linked to the offenses charged, it served the purpose only of conveying to the jury that Huhn's having guns tended to support the testimony that he had a gun when engaged in the charged crimes. We agree." *Id.*

In the present case, any purported probative value is even more tenuous, and thereby more worthy of exclusion. There are no allegations that a shovel was used to commit the charged offenses. Further, there is no assertion that the victim was buried. In *Huhn*, the fact that the defendant bought a gun and a gun (albeit a different one) was used in the commission of the crime apparently created some relevancy issue at the trial level. Here, not even such an insufficient nexus exists. *Blair v. State*, 667 So. 2d 834 (Fla. 4th DCA 1996) (stating that in a burglary conviction, among other charges, the introduction of a briefcase and its contents was improper "because the state failed to show a nexus between the briefcase and its contents to the crimes charged in this case, the prejudicial effect of the items outweighed any probative value," although because defense counsel did not preserve an objection, the court found that the issue was not properly preserved) (citing *Huhn*, 511 So. 2d 583; *Barrett v. State*, 605 So. 2d 560 (Fla. 4th DCA 1992). Because any purported relevancy of testimony related to the shovel would create a danger of unfair prejudice, as there is no sufficient nexus between the shovel and the crimes charged, failing to preclude any related testimony to the shovel would seriously and irreparably undermine Ms. Anthony's right to a fair trial.

7

CONCLUSION

Therefore, in the interests of Casey Marie Anthony's constitutional rights, the Defense respectfully asks this Honorable Court to:

a. Order the Prosecution to file a response motion and memorandum of law within thirty days of the filing of this motion and accompanying memorandum of law;

b. Allow the defense ten business days from the Prosecution's filing of its responsive motion and memorandum of law to file a reply motion and memorandum of law;

c. Set a hearing date, at which time this Honorable Court may hear arguments relating to the motions; and

d. Grant her Motion in Limine to Preclude Certain Testimony of Mr. Brian Burner;

e. If this Honorable Court denies the instant Motion in Limine, Ms. Anthony reserves the right to renew this motion at trial.

Respectfully Submitted,

J. CHENEY MASON, attorney for
CASEY MARIE ANTHONY.

JOSE A. BAEZ, attorney for
CASEY MARIE ANTHONY.

Dated: _Dec. 21_ , 2010

J. CHENEY MASON, ESQUIRE
Florida Bar No.: 131982
390 North Orange Avenue
Suite 2100
Orlando, Florida 32801-1967
Telephone (407) 843-5785
Facsimile (407) 422-6858

8

Once again, however, Judge Perry denied our motion. Despite the inconclusive nature of this "evidence," and the degree to which it contributed to baseless assumptions about the case, it was admitted to the trial. What value this served for justice remains unclear to me; though it certainly gave the prosecution something juicy to parade in front of the cameras.

A particularly emotionally charged area of forensic "evidence" in our case—and an excellent example of the way in which the prejudices that had plagued the case early on continued stubbornly into the trial itself—involved the duct tape found partially adhered to Caylee's head, and the heart-shaped sticker discovered thereafter in the area nearby.

Initially, the child's skeletal remains had been found, with a bit of duct tape adhered to the hair and jaw, within the scattered junk and trash across the street from an elementary school. You may recall that, based on the information related to me by the sheriff while we were both at the television studios—namely, that the child had been found with duct tape wrapped entirely around her head—I had speculated that there would likely be substantial forensic evidence left on the tape. We now know that there was no attached evidence, and that this whole version of the duct-tape story was a distortion, perpetuated in line with media prejudice. It simply suited the story better for the child to have been suffocated with duct tape; but based on this initial distortion, a whole host of secondary distortions followed suit. One can argue back and forth forever as to whether the tape that *was* there had ever been put across Caylee's mouth and nose. But the fact is, there was no evidence to support that conclusion.

The tape in question was *not* wrapped around Caylee's head, but was in fact a small piece, found partially adhered to the hair on one side of her face. No hair, skin, fingerprints, tissue, serology or DNA was ever found on it that could link it either to Caylee or to Casey; no roll or other traces of it—a fairly rare brand—was found either in the car or in the Anthony residence; and as far as real forensic evidence went, its connection with the case was purely accidental. Given the eventual results of the testing, it is far more likely that the duct tape found at the scene was simply used to seal the black plastic bag in which the body was dumped and that it had been moved and shifted as a result of animals pulling the bag apart. Yet the prosecution, carrying on the groundless exaggerations already long circulating about this particular piece of "evidence," would claim even through the trial that it had been used to suffocate Caylee—despite the lack of any of the forensic proofs of this theory that they sought during their investigation.

One of these anxiously sought-after possibilities was that of latent fingerprints. If someone's prints had been identifiable on the tape, it would be inescapable that that person had at least been involved in the disposal of Caylee's body. Now, there are numerous ways to determine the presence of latent fingerprints. It is not limited to the simple technique seen on television, in which a technician uses a soft brush to twirl dust on a surface and then looks for dust adhered to the oil left behind by the ridges of the fingerprints. There are other, far more sophisticated methods used to detect fingerprints—for example, the application of chemical solutions, or the use of ultraviolet lights or high-powered microscopes. The FBI has a number of ways to search for fingerprints, and the adhesive surface of duct tape is particularly easily tested for them. Nevertheless, there were no fingerprints whatsoever found on this duct tape. The prosecution has asserted, and will likely continue to assert, that there must have been fingerprints on it, but that they deteriorated from exposure to the elements. Yet if the prosecution's thesis had been true, that the child's head was at one time entirely wrapped with the tape, fingerprints, or traces of fingerprints, would be expected somewhere.

The other anticipated evidence in relation to this find was DNA; yet despite submissions to the most sophisticated crime labs and technicians available, no DNA was ever found on the duct tape—except some identified as having been left there accidentally by an FBI lab technician. Nor, it seems worthwhile to add, was there any detectable residue of any toxic substance, such as poison or chloroform.

The lengths to which the prosecutorial investigators, in corroboration of the media narrative, would go to fit every detail into their pre-imagined picture were nowhere better illustrated than in the controversy surrounding the heart-shaped sticker also found, adhered to a piece of cardboard, in the vicinity of Caylee's body. Having found this, and presumed a connection between it and the corpse, law enforcement officials searched the Anthony residence from one end to the other, where—naturally enough—they found other heart-shaped stickers.

Parents and grandparents know just how common such stickers are. Little girls everywhere keep them to put on their toys, cards and magazines, walls, shoes, and so forth. Interestingly, the sticker that was found was a thick, dimensional sticker, not a flat one; nothing similar to which, despite a thorough and repeated search, was ever found in the Anthony residence. What was found there were ordinary flat adhesive stickers, which nevertheless, predictably and over objection, were allowed into the trial as evidence following a very strange series of forensic occurrences.

When the piece of duct tape was sent to the FBI lab as a potential "smoking gun," an FBI analyst in their crime lab stated that, in her examination, she saw a distinctly heart-shaped image or impression on the tape. She then ran to alert her supervisor, as she claims, and the two of them immediately attempted to confirm the heart shape on the duct tape. Using almost futuristic electronic equipment, however, neither of them could now see the illusive "impression" that the first examiner claimed to have seen. In the brief interlude between her alleged discovery of the image and her supervisor's attempt to corroborate it, the image had evidently disappeared.

Now, logically one might think that if the examiner had seen anything at all, it was an illusion—a matter of suggestion that had contaminated her thoughts. Where this suggestion had come from is clear enough; it was part of the narrative determined at the scene by the police and propagated by the media in advance of its official adoption by the prosecution themselves. It was part of the overall attempt to fit everything together; which, while a worthwhile effort on the whole, can serve to distort reality as well as explicate it.

With this non-evidence of the link between the heart-shaped sticker and the duct tape, and the original speculation that the tape had indeed been across Caylee's face, the media postulated (as was later argued in trial by the prosecution) that the person who had allegedly affixed the tape over the child's mouth and nose must have been someone close to the child, who was signifying their love for Caylee by putting on a heart-shaped sticker afterward! Thus one speculation proved another, lending an air of truth and clarity to the whole fatuous combination.

It goes without saying that this narrative was soon all but synonymous with the public opinion; but it persisted, and was allowed to persist through the trial, on the side of the prosecutors themselves. The level of indulgence granted to their imaginations was often incredible. At one point they were allowed to have an anthropologist superimpose computer-generated images of tape over computer-morphed pictures of the child and the skull—effectively constructing forensic plausibility for a theory that had no basis in the facts. These images were shown to the jury—along with dramatizations by Mr. Ashton of the suffocating child trying to pull the tape off of her face, while looking at her mother—in an outrageous appeal to their emotions that I could hardly believe the court was willing to allow.

One last bending of the truth on the part of the prosecution's investigative team, perhaps more outrageous even than these imaginative appeals, deserves to be brought to light here.

Seeking any evidence they could to make the tape fit their predetermined explanation, the prosecution asked its forensics teams if there had been any pictures taken of the tape at the site, or scaled measurements made of it, that might confirm their theory.

The e-mailed response was shocking. In essence, the lab replied saying, no, it didn't have any such measurements—but that they might keep that to themselves, by claiming they hadn't taken any pictures, either.

Even I would have had trouble believing this, had I not seen the email for myself; in light of which, I reproduce it here as follows.

LOWE, KAREN K. (LD) (FBI)

From:	MARTIN, ERIN P. (LD) (FBI)
Sent:	Friday, February 06, 2009 2:19 PM
To:	LOWE, KAREN K. (LD) (FBI)
Subject:	tape

<u>UNCLASSIFIED</u>
<u>NON-RECORD</u>

Hey Karen,
  I decided to not give the measurements to Nick that Brian emailed us since it is part of your case notes and it doesn't appear that the jpg's were saved. I didn't want to over step my bounds when it comes to the case notes... I'll just tell Nick that LPOU had no photographs and that TEU has some info on the tape and to discuss w/ you. I don't understand why the ME's office didn't take any scaled photos of the tape when it was on the skull.
epm

<u>UNCLASSIFIED</u>

Now, given that Caylee's remains were discovered in the woods near the family home, it was important for the State prosecution to claim that she had been placed here soon after her death. Had the child been moved at a later time—as from several circumstances it seemed likely she had—this would have been problematic indeed for their case, as Casey Anthony had been in jail during this time.

In an attempt to buttress this presumption, then, the State hired Dr. David Hall, a retired botanist from Gainesville, Florida, to provide "expert" testimony in regards to the discovery site. The defense team spent days analyzing Dr. Hall's opinions and were left somewhat flabbergasted at the conclusions that he was willing to advance.

Dr. Hall claimed, in a report he authored, that he could determine roughly how long Caylee's remains had been in one location by measuring the diameter of the roots that had grown through some of the fabric of the girl's clothing. This, like most spotty forensics, sounds reasonable enough; but there were numerous problems with Dr. Hall's claims. One of the most glaring weaknesses in his argument was that he was unable to identify the plant that had sent out the roots in question. This, as it turns out, poses a very serious problem to his theory, since plants—even plants of the same species and in the same environment—can grow at widely different rates. There are, Dr. Hall admitted, between sixty and eighty thousand different types of plants that grow in Florida, some of which grow much more quickly than others. This growth rate also varies with other factors, such as season, access to sun, access to shade, access to nutrients, the effect of animals and that of nearby competing plants. Dr. Hall had not been cognizant of any of these factors in his examination; indeed, he had never seen the roots at issue in person. He had only seen the photographs of them that were given to him and had no knowledge as to whether these photographs had been enlarged, or how close the scale ruler was to the lens of the camera—factors that can very easily distort perceptions of size in photographs.

Still more suspicion-inducing was Dr. Hall's confession that though he had authored a book on botany, nowhere in publication had he ever detailed, or recommended, this root-measuring procedure. He further admitted that in his years of teaching botany he had never taught the procedure he was now allowing to be relied upon as evidence. His method had in fact never been taught or applied as an appropriate method of analysis by anyone, at any time, anywhere; nor had claims like his ever been accepted by any court. There was not a single published article that he could refer to and confirm that supported him; when he was questioned under oath in a deposition about his opinion and methodology, he responded, "I don't have any standard—just experience."

Under some circumstances, such a grounds for conclusion might be allowable, but not in a capital murder trial. If there are no standards, then a witness can claim anything he or she wants to—or that someone else wants them to. There is no way to cross-examine such a witness, or determine an incidence of error for them. For there to be reliable "science," especially of a forensic kind, there have to be controls, the explicit recognition both of false positives and false negatives, the application of reliable methods.

Dr. Hall, on the contrary, had to acknowledge—when cross-examined by the defense in a deposition that varied widely from his prosecutorial testimony—that he had never even experimented with his hypothesis to test its reliability, much less subjected it to third-party analysis, before offering it as prosecutorial evidence. Given this admission, we were astonished that the prosecution would even consider advancing such specious stuff; and accordingly, months before the trial, the defense filed a number of motions to exclude this and other parts of the prosecution's testimony.

Ultimately, *Frye* hearings were held on the subject. A *Frye* hearing is a legal proceeding in which one party to a dispute makes the claim that an expert witness for the other side is asserting unscientific claims. The practice is based on a 1923 Federal Appeals Court decision, in which one of the prosecution's "experts" testified that he had administered a lie-detector test based on the defendant's blood pressure. The court refused to admit this test as evidence, finding that a scientific principle requires recognition and general acceptance in its field.

By now, however, most states and the federal courts have done away with the "*Frye* standard," using a newer one called the *Daubert* standard. This standard, based in civil cases, does not necessarily require general acceptance by other experts in the scientific community, but makes the judge's satisfaction the measure of reliability. (Since this writing, the Florida Supreme Court has adopted the *Daubert* standard.) What this meant in our case was that, despite the inability of the prosecution and Dr. Hall to produce a single publication or alternate expert who might corroborate Dr. Hall's claims, these claims were admitted by the court as evidence and allowed to be presented as solid forensic science. We found this particularly disillusioning, given the fact that in Florida, there are explicit rules requiring that novel forensic claims be proven reliable on some other basis than simply the opinion of the witness who attempts to get them accepted as evidence.

Fortunately, by that time the defense had consulted with a genuine expert in the field, who refuted Dr. Hall's conclusions unequivocally. Dr. Jane Bock is a retired professor emeritus at the University of Colorado and a nationally known forensic botanist. She has worked on a number of high profile cases, including the JonBenét Ramsey case. At the time of the Casey Anthony trial, Dr. Bock had authored over eighty-five publications and had a reputation as a straight shooter who was often consulted by law enforcement and prosecution officials.

Stunned as she was by Dr. Hall's claims, Dr. Bock tried initially to give him the benefit of the doubt. He had to have something to back up such far-reaching claims, she reasoned; indeed, she was concerned that she herself, despite all of her experience, had perhaps overlooked something. She spent weeks trying to find even a single article in support of Dr. Hall's methodology. All she could find was the established fact that such determinations required a knowledge of what kind of plant a root came from, and a continued measurement of the root and plant over time as they grew. In this manner you could obtain the growth rate of that single plant—but not the whole species, because of all the other variable influences on growth previously outlined.

After numerous first-hand inspections of the plant material in question and the site itself—in addition to the photographs upon which Dr. Hall's claims were solely based—Dr. Bock testified not only that Dr. Hall's claims were thoroughly unscientific in nature, but that it was clear that the remains of the child had most likely been placed in the area within days or weeks of the discovery.

She also acknowledged that coyotes could have carried away parts of the remains, which elicited one of Mr. Ashton's more unintentionally humorous responses of the trial. Having dared to present the court with such baldly unscientific forensic evidence as the foregoing, he now scoffed at the botanical expert on the stand, dismissing the idea of coyotes even being in the state. The animal had lately become an infamous nuisance in Florida, as any Florida resident might have told him. Hardly surprising, really, that a man with so patent a disdain for scientific truth should show himself so blatantly ignorant of reality in his own home state!

8

The Search for Truth, or for an Excuse?

Those who were aware of the local and national news media broadcasts surrounding the "Case Against Casey" could not have missed the hordes of people searching for little Caylee. Given the public interest, bolstered every fifteen to thirty minutes by teaser advertisements on the news, it wasn't too surprising to see how many people would participate in the search.

That public awareness is invaluable when a child is missing is something nobody would dispute. The problem is when the news media uses this opportunity to promote their programs and commercial interests. In Caylee's case, it would have been enough simply to make an announcement, or series of announcements, that a search was being organized, along with the appropriate requests for help and proper phone numbers to call. Appalling as it was, however, selfish motives asserted themselves alongside this more wholesome objective very early on—not only in the media, but among those who showed up to take part in the search.

Immediately upon the media "release" of Cindy Anthony's hysterical 911 call and the details of Caylee's disappearance, the hysterical siege began. People were soon looking everywhere for Caylee, many hoping to enjoy a reward. One of the detectives working on the case reported that law enforcement received some 6,000 tips from callers alleging to have sighted Caylee. Believe it or not, despite the discovery of Caylee's body and the subsequent trial, there are those who continue to report such sightings. Even during the writing of this book I have received several e-mails from people who are absolutely certain that Caylee is alive and that they know where she is. Unfortunately, whenever one of these Samaritans reported a sighting to law enforcement during the search, resources had to be expended in investigating it. The majority of these claims were so ridiculous and impossible as to defy logic; nevertheless, they flooded in.

In the midst of this process, Cindy and George Anthony were contacted by a search company called Texas Equusearch, a supposedly nonprofit organization that sends volunteers out in search of missing people. A lawyer who had insinuated himself into the case with the Anthonys brought in this company to help with the search; later, after the Anthonys terminated his services, he went on to represent Texas Equusearch—going so far as to solicit, and apparently obtain, a "waiver of conflict" from the Anthonys in order to keep himself on the case.

In any event, Texas Equusearch officials then came to town and began using the media to notify the general public that they were seeking volunteers to participate in the search for little Caylee. Hundreds of people volunteered—some from very far distances out of state, others from down the street.

These volunteers, we were rather surprised to learn, were each required to sign applications to be "searchers" with Texas Equusearch, and to pay the company a $25.00 fee to join the search. Allegedly the fee was to offset the administrative costs and expenses incurred by this "non-profit" organization; nevertheless, the Orange County Sheriff's Department contributed an additional $30,000 to the company to help "seed the search." Volunteers were not required to undergo any form of background check, training or education whatsoever; they simply had to be live bodies prepared to go around looking. Still, initially one might have thought this was a good thing; it seemed likely they had find the child soon.

They mounted a huge search plan, creating teams with assigned leaders who themselves had no qualification, other than the fact that they were first to sign up for a particular group. Under this makeshift leadership, hundreds and hundreds of volunteers began to search in and around the Central Florida lakes, rivers, woods, swamps, parks and anywhere else a body might be concealed.

The media was, of course, omnipresent throughout these efforts, which were broadcast on television daily until they began to resemble a form of stage performance. News crews would go to a particular location designated beforehand for the search of the day and film the volunteers as they walked through the different areas, intently poking sticks in the ground and looking in every direction they could. Searchers worked throughout the day and night, some stopping to be interviewed by the excited press from time to time, others leaving off their day's search, only to take up position demonstrating in front of the Anthony household.

The search included law enforcement personnel and volunteers in helicopters, on all-terrain vehicles and on horseback. People walking, people with cameras, media personalities and general curiosity-seekers swarmed by the droves. Yet despite the remarkable intensity of the search effort, it would be some time before the child's body was found—in one of the first locations where searchers had looked in vain.

The site where Caylee Anthony's remains would be discovered is now well known. It is a lightly wooded area slightly more than seventeen feet from the paved edge of Suburban Drive, a street that intersects with the Anthonys' street only about a quarter of a mile from their residence. In the beginnings of the search it had not taken much to suspect that foul play of some kind had befallen Caylee, and to conclude that the search ought to begin in the nearest possible disposal area. Accordingly, the area around Suburban Drive was one of the first to be searched. Yet at the time it was first looked over, nothing was found there.

On August the 11th of 2008, a meter reader named Roy Kronk was doing some routine work out by an elementary school on Suburban Drive. While on the job site he felt the call of nature, and rather than leave to find a public restroom, he went into the woods. It was a somewhat isolated area, and there weren't any people around to catch him in the act.

There, Mr. Kronk claims, he stumbled upon the skull that would turn out to be Caylee Anthony's. Emerging from the woods, he excitedly mentioned it to a co-worker and, later, to his roommate. He called the sheriff's department immediately to report the sighting—and they didn't respond.

Remember, at this point there were thousands of "sightings" and tips coming in, and hundreds of active searchers swirling around everywhere trying to find the child. This was the lead news story of every media organization in the country. Yet the sheriff's department did nothing! Mr. Kronk, naturally enough, was befuddled. He couldn't believe that the sheriff was ignoring him. He wasn't just some kook; he worked for the county and had identified himself as a county employee. When nothing was done in response to his call, Mr. Kronk called the sheriff's department again on the 12th of August, and yet again on the 13th. Finally a deputy appeared to meet him, and Mr. Kronk pointed out the area where he had seen the skull. But instead of taking Mr.

Kronk's disclosure seriously and evaluating the significance of his sighting, the deputy scolded him, making it clear that he didn't believe him, and left.

The sheriff's office continued to do nothing about Mr. Kronk's sighting. They didn't even report it to their media collaborators. There were news trucks and camera crews amongst the other curiosity-seekers and searchers within a hundred yards. There was no shortage of people that would have been on hands and knees, if necessary, searching the area for what Mr. Kronk claimed to have seen. But they did not investigate the sighting at all, and the search continued—all through Central Florida, the rest of the state and who knows how far outside of it. False sightings continued, and theories abounded.

Of course, during all this time, Casey Anthony was either in jail or out on bond under 24/7 supervision. It's very clear, even to the most skeptical "Casey hater," that she could not herself have planted the remains of her child in the area off Suburban Drive during the period of time between the sighting by Mr. Kronk and their official discovery in December—and this would become critically important later.

On December the 11th of 2008, Mr. Kronk went back to the same area where he had reported his discovery to the police back in August. He went straight back to where he had been before, and there again he saw the skull. In his sworn testimony, which there is no reason to doubt, he indicated that he held out his meter-reader stick, inserted it into the empty orbital socket of the skull and lifted it some four feet off the ground. He then put it back down and ran out to again report his find to law enforcement.

This time the police responded and Caylee Anthony's remains were officially found.

Now, during the period of time that intervened between Roy Kronk's first and second sightings of the skull, there had been untold numbers of searchers in the same area who had somehow never found the child's remains there. It is hard to imagine that so many people with the same design and desire could search that area so fruitlessly—especially when you look at the site diagram below.

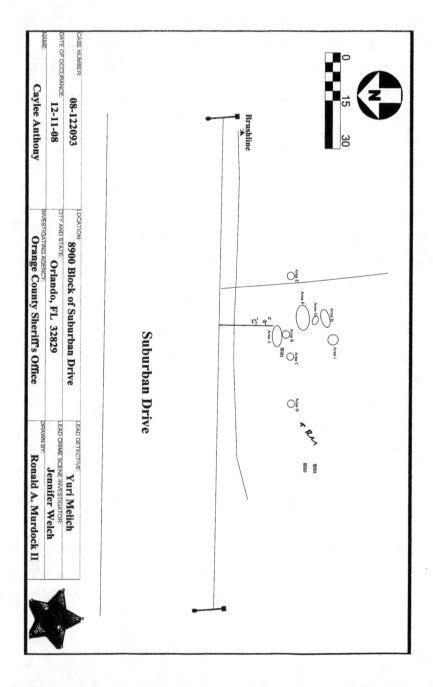

Be that as it may, now the forensic investigation of the site could begin. Crime-scene investigators were soon on the scene, and the area was searched methodically. The soil was sifted, and every inch of the area was photographed. Dozens of skilled forensic technicians worked busily, essentially around the clock. The whole area was cordoned off and guarded. The news media was kept back—at least a few feet; from which they surrounded the scene with all manner of speculations, conclusions, conjectures and outright fabrications.

Casey, of course, remained in jail during this time, and as part of its investigation, the sheriff's department concocted a new scheme to try to illegally elicit some form of spontaneous confession from her, behind the back of her legal cousel. They decided to bring Casey out of her cell and place her in an infirmary area within the jail, where there was a television that she could view and video cameras they could train on her to monitor her every gesture and sound. Then they would conduct a *de facto* interrogation, while subjecting the young mother to a viewing of the shocking discovery of her child's remains.

That this behavior on the part of the sheriff's department was as inhumane as it was conniving is hardly to be argued against, considering the fact that Casey was not yet (as she was not ever) proven guilty. They could have asked the jail chaplain, a nurse or—God forbid—her lawyer to inform her of the discovery; but then, that wouldn't provide the fodder for emotional condemnation that her candid reaction to that situation might. Accordingly, Casey was seated in the waiting area of the infirmary while the sheriff's department, having conspired with the news media to play the story on-air of the finding of Caylee's remains, surreptitiously videotaped her watching it. Unsurprisingly, Casey was suddenly in great distress at the news. She doubled over and hyperventilated; which the news media, for their part in the conspiracy, were allowed to broadcast for the world to see.

The assumption made by many, that Casey's reaction had been from guilt, ignores the fact that she was now suddenly confronted with the reality of the loss of her child. Months of speculation and accusation had now come down to an in-your-face confrontation, and it would be hard to imagine a parent dealing with such abrupt news of the death of their child in any kind of decorous manner. It also didn't seem to strike many people that this was a situation in which Casey's show of grief was apparently condemnatory of her, whereas in many others she had been similarly condemned for not showing *enough* grief. To many people the woman was simply guilty, regardless what she did. This self-contradiction notwithstanding, the malicious local media personalities had a frenzied field day with the tapes—and they weren't the only ones.

Recall that it is a well known rule of evidence under Florida and federal law that even such evidence as might be probative of something relevant to a case can nevertheless be excluded, and should be excluded, from trial if the prejudice it is likely to elicit outweighs any probative value it may have. Now, all this video of Casey's reaction really proved is that she had been taken into the infirmary, set down in front of a television and shown the broadcast of Caylee's discovery, whereupon she had become seriously distressed and hyperventilated. It did not prove anything else in the case, *unless* we allow proof based on nothing but conjecture to be admissible. Apparently Judge Perry thought this was the case, however, and admitted even this "evidence" to trial.

Now, some of the facts of the case had come together. There was no longer a need to speculate about whether the child was alive, kidnapped, or in some other way inexplicably missing. Now the State would not have to try to prove Casey guilty of first-degree murder without a body, or the ability to prove the cause and manner of death. Given this new state of things, the State wasted no time in reneging on its previous waiver of its pursuit of the death penalty, and now sought it in earnest.

The Medical Examiner's investigator and assistants retrieved the remains as they were found and took them to the medical examiner's office. The bones had to be studied and put back together, since wild animals had evidently moved some of them; and anthropologists were called in to identify the various bones and distinguish them, in some instances, from those of other small animals. The Chief Medical Examiner, having returned to Orlando to take charge of the investigation, hastened to have face time with the various news organizations already surrounding her office.

Considering the remarkable intensity of search efforts, the defense team was curious as to how Caylee's remains could have remained undiscovered during the period between August the 11th and December the 11th of 2008. We were equally curious to know how a man like Roy Kronk, whose participation in the search had been accidental and his testimony offered entirely in good faith, could testify one way as to what he found, yet be controverted out-of-hand by officials who claimed that it had been found differently. I, for one, could not think of any possible reason Mr. Kronk might have to lie about what he found; nor was any substantial reason ever offered in the case.

So what exactly had happened during those four months? We knew, from the reports and discovery provided, about the enormous number of people and amount of equipment that had been involved in the search and of the extent to which the area in question had been searched to no avail before the final revelation of Caylee's remains. We had reports from the sheriff's department indicating that there had been a search there by law enforcement with no results; we knew that Texas Equusearch had also been brought in, and that its volunteers had also searched the area with no results. Whether Roy Kronk had or had not found the remains back in August, the State still had a major problem: during those intervening four months, the remains had evidently not been there; and Casey, who had been in jail or under 24/7 observation during all this time, could not possibly have moved them to where they were eventually found. The inescapable conclusion in this case was that somebody else had to have done it; so it became important to the defense to hear from those in particular who had searched the area without finding anything.

When our pursuit of the identities of the volunteer searchers intensified, believe it or not, we were faced with objections and opposition by Texas Equusearch and its lawyer. Among the absurd claims espoused by the company was that its searchers had a right to privacy that should be protected. They did not want to be identified, the company claimed, as having participated in the search, as they had searched simply as conscientious citizens, in confidence and in good faith.

Now, we will never know the exact motives of the hundreds of searchers, but there is no question that this claim to their wish for privacy and confidentiality is nonsense. If the people searching wanted to do so privately and anonymously, why did they parade back and forth before numerous television cameras and reporters, and even pause to grant them personal interviews? Why did they sign applications providing their names, addresses and phone numbers to participate in the search to begin with? Not only fame, but a quarter-million-dollar reward lay in wait for the person who found Caylee; and of this fact, nobody was unaware. Could any reasonable person think that they could collect upon such high stakes and be kept anonymous?

A formal request was made by the co-counsel for the identities of the searchers. The objections and obstruction by Texas Equusearch and their lawyer continued, with the collaboration of the prosecution and the court. The prosecutor, Ms. Burdick, was allowed to review these so-called "private" Texas Equusearch documents, and reported that she could only identify thirty-two volunteers who had searched on Suburban Drive, possibly including the relevant area. I refused to accept this as a fact; there had simply been too many people caught on television cameras and observed by witnesses from all walks of life for me to believe that only been thirty-two searchers had been through that site. After some skirmishing back and forth, an arrangement was made to allow Mr. Baez and me to go to the Texas Equusearch lawyer's office and search through the files to identify other relevant witnesses. Under the conditions of our agreement, we had to pay a representative of the Texas Equusearch company to oversee our review of them. I was annoyed by this process, and found its implications professionally insulting, but did not want to waste any more time in arguing about it.

When we arrived at the lawyer's conference room for our inspection, we found the Texas Equusearch monitor waiting for us with four boxes on the conference table. A couple of these were file boxes in some semblance of order; the others were stained, ripped and disheveled, as though the company had taken, at best, only a cursory care of its records. I reached for the first box of documents, opened the lid, and was immediately told, "No, you can't look at that box." The box was then taken abruptly and put out of the way.

After all the motions, letters and gnashing of teeth it had required to get us the opportunity to look at these documents, this was particularly puzzling; but I brushed it aside and reached for the second box. Incredibly, the monitor took this box away as well. Now we were left with two boxes to look at. Mr. Baez began looking through one, and I the other, and within about thirty minutes I had identified well over fifty relevant searchers, just from the box that I was inspecting. So much for the prosecution's claim of thirty-two.

About that time, Mr. Baez looked around and saw that a camera crew had gathered in the reception area of the lawyer's office and had trained a camera on us through the glass doors to record our search of the boxes. It became evident that the Texas Equusearch lawyer had arranged for the media to show up to monitor and observe what we were doing in an effort to aggrandize his office. I was appalled. This was so unprofessional and outrageous in my opinion that it ended the search, and we returned to court.

At the subsequent hearing, when we presented the court with what had happened during our "inspection," the court did—albeit with some reluctance and over continued objection—allow us to re-inspect the documents; but now we had to do it in the courthouse, in a courtroom, with an appointed Special Master to oversee what was being done. We then gathered in the assigned courtroom: the Texas Equusearch representatives, their secretaries and the like, and their files, plus me, my young colleague Lisabeth Fryer and our investigators. Files were handed to us one at a time so that we could look at the volunteer sign-up sheets and start calling the volunteers.

We were unable to reach more than half of the people listed in these files; yet still, we identified and confirmed 161 searchers who acknowledged that they had searched Suburban Drive during the time period in question.

Once we had the identity of these 161 witnesses, we began to follow up by calling, and on some occasions visiting, them to discuss their potential testimonies. We asked them a number of questions, specifically whether they had searched the area where the remains were found, and whether they had taken any pictures to corroborate their story. During this process we heard a number of interesting testimonies. One of the people identified as having searched the area, whose identity had not been previously disclosed to the defense, told us that when he had wanted to search the area where Caylee's body was found, he was told by the sheriff's department that they had already searched it and that he could not. Another pair of young men, whom I referred to as the "Kissimmee boys," acknowledged that they had spent a great deal of time and energy in searching that area, by all-terrain vehicle as well as on foot, and had found nothing.

Unfortunately, however, some of these people had already been "wood-shedded" by the prosecution's detectives by the time the defense's investigators got to them—meaning they had been confronted, intimidated and, in some cases, outright threatened. They were told unequivocally not only that they did not have to talk to the defense or the defense's investigators, but that the prosecution preferred they didn't. One would hope more of these people would simply advise the detectives that they had only intended to tell the truth, but in fact many of them were successfully silenced by these goon-like tactics.

It is the job of the defense to thoroughly investigate and explore the facts. For a prosecutor or a law enforcement operative to try to keep witnesses secret, or keep them from cooperating with the defense, is a clear and simple obstruction of justice that is not only illegal, but reprehensible. But in our case, even this degree of obstruction was not enough for the prosecution. Not satisfied with trying to hide the names and identities of the searchers, instructing them to not cooperate with the defense, and trying to intimidate them out of assisting in simple fact-finding, they went on to threaten to charge more than one witness with a crime for doing so.

One of the team leaders in this case, a young man who had volunteered for Texas Equusearch, was certain that he had searched the area where the remains were found. He was interviewed by one of our investigators in the presence of his lawyer. He was quite specific in his testimony, both as to the area he had searched, and the time he had searched it.

Unfortunately, during this interview the witness had a digital recorder on his person. There are many state jurisdictions that would have had no problem with this, but it is one of the fine points of Florida law that you cannot surreptitiously record anybody's conversation without their permission, unless you are a law enforcement agent doing so in an official investigation or pursuant to a court order. It was later discovered by the prosecution that he had surreptitiously recorded the interview; and even though the two people whose conversation was secretly recorded—our investigator and his lawyer—had signed statements that waived any concern of privacy or objection, the State took the occasion to eliminate this very strong testimony from the side of the defense, threatening the young man with prosecution until he agreed to change his testimony about having searched the area in the first place.

I filed a motion with the court to have the recording produced so that we could hear it and go on from there with establishing the credibility of the witness. I reproduce that motion as follows; at this point one might guess the results easily enough.

IN THE CIRCUIT COURT OF THE NINTH JUDICIAL CIRCUIT
IN AND FOR ORANGE COUNTY, FLORIDA

STATE OF FLORIDA,

    Plaintiff,

v.

CASEY MARIE ANTHONY,

    Defendant.
_____/

CASE NO.: 48-2008-CF-0015606-O
DIVISION: 16
Hon. Stan Strickland

**DEFENDANT'S MOTION TO COMPEL PRODUCTION OF
TAPE RECORDED STATEMENT OF JOE JORDAN**

COMES NOW the Defendant, CASEY MARIE ANTHONY, by and through her undersigned attorneys, and moves this Court to enter its Order compelling the state of Florida, by and through its prosecuting authorities in this cause, to produce a certain tape recording of an interview with witness Joe Jordan to the defense, and as grounds therefore shows:

1. On December 9, 2009 the prosecution in this case informed this Court that they were in possession of a tape which was surreptitiously made by Joe Jordan while he was being interviewed by defense investigator Mort Smith in the presence of Mr. Jordan's lawyer, Mr. Kelly Sims. That interview took place on October 27, 2009.

2. At that time, the State asked to be relieved of their responsibility to turn that tape over to the defense, because it was taken in violation of Florida Statute 934.03.

3. Mr. Smith has reviewed the police interviews with Mr. Jordan, which occurred after his interview, and has determined that the statements to the police differ substantially from what was said in his lawyer's office. *See* Affidavit of Mort Smith, attached.

4. Among other things, Mr. Jordan, in the presence of his attorney, Mr. Sims, revealed to defense investigator Smith that he, (Jordan), had personally searched the ground

area where ultimately the remains of the victim, Caylee Anthony, were found, and that the area was dry in September of 2008. More importantly, Mr. Jordan confirms that during his search of that area there was no body there and no evidence of animal activity or other indications that the victim's remains were in the place where subsequently they were alleged to have been found for the second time by Mr. Kronk.

5. Both Mr. Sims and Mr. Smith have declined to seek any prosecution of Mr. Jordan for the surreptitious recording and potential violations of Florida law. Accordingly, Mr. Jordan is not in legal jeopardy.

6. The "exculpatory nature" of this evidence should be obvious. The Defendant, at all potentially material times related to the discovery of her daughter's remains, was in custody and, accordingly, could not have placed her daughter's remains where they were located by Mr. Kronk. Eye witness testimony to the absence of such remains and in that location conclusively establishes that some other person than the Defendant had to have placed the child's remains where they were found.

7. While there may technically be a violation of Florida Statute 934.03, since neither of the aggrieved parties desire prosecution, this Court can order the production of this tape recording as a clearly exculpatory statement. Any statute, such as 934.03, must give way to the Constitutional Rights of a person facing a criminal charge and the potential death sentence, which is being sought by the State. *See for example Lee v. Kemna*, 534 U.S. 362 (2002) and *Davis v. Alaska*, 415 U.S. 308 (1974)[1].

8. This Court is simultaneously considering defense Motions to compel full disclosure

---

[1] If need be, this Court can exercise its supervisory authority and grant Mr. Jordan immunity from prosecution under *Kastigar v. United States*, 406 U.S. 441 (1972) theory, or order the State to do so.

of all search records from Equusearch. which have been opposed by that company. The surfacing of witness Jordan. and now the disclosure of the recording involved. additionally supports the contention that all of the Equusearch records must be turned over for the defense to view and for the defense to determine the values thereof.

WHEREFORE. the Defendant prays this Court enter its Order compelling the prosecution in this cause to turn over to the defense the entirety of the tape recorded statement made by Mr. Jordan on October 27. 2009.

CERTIFICATE OF SERVICE

I HEREBY CERTIFY that a true and correct copy of the foregoing Notice of Appearance has been furnished by hand delivery to the Office of the State Attorney.415 N. Orange Avenue. Orlando. Florida 32801 this _2nd_ day of April. 2010.

J. CHENEY MASON. ESQ.
Florida Bar No.: 0131982
J. CHENEY MASON. P.A.
390 N. Orange Avenue. Suite 2100
Orlando. Florida 32801
Telephone: 407-843-5785
Facsimile: 407-422-6858
One of the attorneys for Defendant

Upon hearing our motion, the prosecutor claimed that she had not listened to the recorded conversation because that would be "using it," which she felt would have been a wrongful act on her part—even a crime. Absurd as this was, it was good enough for the judge, who denied us access to this valuable evidence. As a result, the witness was free to change his story and say whatever the prosecutors asked him to say.

The treatment of that witness was reprehensible enough. But it wasn't as bad as what they did to yet another team leader, a woman that had come in from out of state. She was so strong in her testimony that she was able to provide photographs that showed her with an investigator and a defense team lawyer standing in the spot where the remains had been found. She was absolutely positive that she had gone to that specific spot before, she said, and informed all who cared to hear that she and her team members had searched it with no results.

Under Florida Criminal Procedure, the defense's taking the sworn deposition testimony of a witness opens that witness to reciprocal deposition questioning by the prosecution. In this case the witness's prosecutorial deposition was taken via Skype, because she was in New York. She had been intimidated and threatened by law enforcement before and had lawyered up with a very well known and experienced defense lawyer to make sure her rights would be protected.

The prosecutor, not wanting to be confused by any evidence or information not conforming to her theory, assumed that this witness was lying for some reason and asked her to produce documents to prove that she had been part of the Texas Equusearch team. Accordingly, the witness faxed new copies of these documents to the prosecution—which the defense team already had, and had given to the prosecution in advance of her deposition.

One might think this would close that particular objection to her testimony. But the prosecution, in collusion with the Texas Equusearch representative, claimed that the documents must be some form of forgery, on the grounds that the prosecution had not found them in their private search of the records—the very search the defense had not been allowed to conduct. The prosecution then began to threaten the witness, informing her that destruction of or tampering with evidence in a capital murder case could net her thirty years in prison. They continued to harass and intimidate her, despite her producing a perfectly legitimate rationale for why the documents had not been present for them to find earlier; in the end, deciding it was not worth it to subject yet another innocent person to malicious and false prosecution, the defense team elected not to use her as a witness.

Our search of the searchers had at least established that there were a great many people who had combed the discovery area without finding the remains. There were credible witnesses, maps, drawings and photographs to that effect. To counteract this overwhelming evidence, the prosecution came up with a new answer. Since there was no question that searches of the area had been conducted in vain, they reasoned, the specific area in which the remains were located must have been underwater at the time the searchers came through, and so had gone unsearched.

In pursuing this theory, the prosecutors went so far as to hire a hydrologist from the University of Florida, who was brought in to inspect, survey and study the searched area. In the sworn deposition testimony of this expert, he explained in great detail how he had taken soil borings and measured water depths in the nearest waterway. He had consulted maps and elevation charts, planted instruments to measure the water table and so on; and much to the State's surprise, it was his opinion that, at the time in question, the area had *not* been underwater.

Not to be distracted by the truth, the State stepped up its campaign of influencing as many of the 161 witnesses as they could. They explained the problem and managed to "encourage" witnesses to remember that when they had searched the area, it had in fact been underwater; and over and over again, this routine played out. Witnesses were subpoenaed and brought in by the prosecution; shown pictures of woods that could have been anywhere; and made to believe that if they couldn't distinguish one tree from another, perhaps they had made a mistake as to the specific area of search and that, therefore, the remains might have been there after all. It is disturbing, the degree to which people's allegiance to the truth, and even to the testimony of their own memory, can be affected by authoritative coercion, but so it is—and no less in capital cases than in those of lighter consequence.

9

Freedom of the Press

When I was a young lawyer, there were no cameras allowed in the courtrooms. Instead, reporters sat in, listened to testimonies and took notes. Interviews could be held outside the courthouse and were often conducted by conscientious and well-meaning professionals. In the early '70s and into the '80s there was a reporter in Orlando, Mr. Dick Burdette, who was notably methodical in his pursuit of accuracy. He would make appointments to meet with people and ask questions; he would attend hearings; he would research what he was talking about, and try to fully understand it; then he would write meaningful stories and undistorted articles presenting his findings to the public. I fear that his breed is all but gone today.

There are still some reporters that strive to report objectively in their broadcasts, but time crunches associated with competitive news deadlines and—more importantly—commercial sponsorship needs have changed everything about their job. Many of them are no longer journalists at all—for the most part, they are entertainers. Shortcuts take precedence in their industry over hard work and accuracy, and the law enforcement community and state prosecutors have learned how to turn this new and increasingly superficial news media to their advantage.

Law enforcement agencies now routinely have full-time spokespersons and publicists, who create news releases and press announcements to be distributed and made available to the distracted entertainers posing as journalists. Why inquire about the opinions of a lawyer on the other side of a favorite theory? Why waste time reading into a case's history, or spending hours in court observing its slow-moving proceedings? All one needs to do nowadays is stop by the State Attorney's office, pick up a copy of the press release of the day and concoct a story on that basis.

Ironically, these days the news media surrounding court cases are frequently of the opinion that their role is so important that they require special treatment, as though they were one of the parties to the lawsuit, and law enforcement agencies are all too happy to foster this misperception. As I mentioned before, in Florida, the Public Records Act is one of the chief sources of encouragement for this outrageous abuse of the First Amendment. Recall that under this series of laws, any person can write a letter of demand to a governmental agency—be it the prosecutors, the sheriff or the police—requesting access to all documents and records pertaining to a particular person or subject, and the law enforcement community decides what they will give up. If they don't want to reveal something, they simply deny the request by saying the investigation is ongoing. However, if they want to poison the well of public opinion, they will parcel information out to the news media that serves their particular interests. Thus, under the aegis of transparency and public awareness, the truth is routinely distorted and manipulated in the public eye.

Similarly, I have heard people try to justify the presence of cameras in the courtroom with the argument that they're used to educate the public and reveal the truth of what goes on there. This is a sensible enough notion of their use, but unfortunately, one somewhat at variance with reality. Nowadays cameras left in the courtroom will record a whole day's occurrences, only five to seven seconds of which is presented to the public—typically as the setting for a reporter's saying whatever he or she wants to say, in line with a predetermined agenda. Supporters of cameras in the courtroom, having recourse simply to the sacrosanctity of "First Amendment rights," tend to ignore the increased artificiality that such excerpted footage makes possible.

I myself have participated in the trials of more than a dozen criminal cases that were televised from the courtroom; in every single one of these circumstances I have observed a change in demeanor of the judges when they were filmed. It is easy to forget that they are politicians who will eventually be running for reelection, and that, despite the serious nature of their jobs, they are in fact no different from any other politician in terms of their reliance upon public perception.

The lawyers in these cases, I have found, are often terrified of how they may be portrayed in the thirty-second news stories that follow their day in court and behave stiffly when the cameras are rolling. The wise ones, recognizing that what they say and do is going to be taken out of context anyway, try to ignore them altogether.

Witnesses, too, tend to behave differently when cameras are present. They dress up in their Sunday best; many go to the trouble of having their hair styled for the occasion. While it's nice to see people treating what are indeed solemn proceedings with respect, it is often humorous, and sometimes a little off-putting, to see the theatrical attitudes they adopt and spread to one another under these circumstances. Nor are jurors immune to the same contagion, despite the fact that in many cases television cameras are not allowed to record them or broadcast their faces or voices. They still come to the courtroom prepared for possible coverage and exposure—and this kind of media influence may be the most alarming of all.

During this next phase of the "Case Against Casey," the media was everywhere: inside and outside the courthouse, up and down the streets, hovering overhead in helicopters. They even followed the lawyers into restrooms.

I'm told different numbers by court administration authorities, but apparently in this case approximately six hundred media outlets sought and obtained credentials to be able to observe and report on the trial. Every hearing involved, no matter how trivial or innocuous, was attended by news agencies competing for the next scoop—or the next occasion to invent one. In their rush to be first to publish the latest on the case, these agencies often rang false alarms, and were taken in by some very strange deceptions.

One evening, I was called at home by Mr. Tony Pipitone, a news reporter from the CBS affiliate Channel 6. I had known him as a generally competent man, who at least attempted to be factually accurate in his reporting. Mr. Pipitone wanted to know if there was any truth to the news that Casey Anthony had fired Jose Baez as her lawyer. Naturally, I was amazed and asked him where he had heard this story.

It turned out that a creative inmate serving a lengthy prison sentence in another state had filed a pleading in the Circuit Court to the effect that Casey had wanted to get rid of Mr. Baez for an assortment of reasons, including incompetency and inexperience. There was not an inkling of truth to this report; it was simply the fabrication of a guy doing time, with nothing better to occupy his mind. Mr. Pipitone had the sense to see through these sham claims and had called me to verify the story before he ran with it—but more than a few of his colleagues did not have his circumspection, and soon the rumor was on the TV news and even in the paper.

The disturbing thing about this whole situation from a legal perspective was that the author of the motion was not an attorney in any capacity, and thus could not have signed his name with an official Bar Association number, which is required to file such motions in court. I heard from a member of the clerk's office that this was not the first time this ruse had been tried; yet how this one had gotten through is an unsettling mystery.

Soon the distorted stories being circulated, along with prosecutorial speculations leaked intentionally to the media, brought national attention to the case. In my opinion the single most dangerously vituperative personality present for it all was none other than Nancy Grace. By all accounts, the Casey Anthony trial really put Ms. Grace's nationally broadcasted show on the map; and when it had ended, her popularity dropped noticeably. Every night this woman would rail vehemently and emotionally against any suggestion of Casey's innocence and do everything in her power to increase the likelihood of a conviction. Ms. Grace claimed to have been a former prosecuting attorney herself, and, therefore, to know what she was talking about; but though she was indeed, for a short period of time, a prosecutor, her expertise in that capacity is open to considerable question.

Another news personality on the same network, Jane Velez-Mitchell, seemed a second Nancy Grace, and every night the two of them would headline the "Case Against Casey" in the most bald-facedly prejudicial fashion. Whenever either of them managed to get somebody on their show who wanted to speak reasonably and objectively about what was going on, as soon as that person expressed an opinion inconsistent with either of theirs, they were cut off.

Some of these "expert" guests were in fact experienced lawyers; though in the media's frenzied pursuit of new material, it did get to the point where any lawyer self-aggrandizing enough to buy or rent space on billboards was instantly recognized as a "prominent expert." Local news agencies seeking ready sound bites from local lawyers cared only minimally about the qualifications of the people they were tapping for their interviews. It didn't matter whether the alleged expert had ever tried a homicide case; nor whether they had ever attained or qualified to test for Board certification. All they needed was a law degree and a willingness to jump in front of the camera.

One of the most offensive and outrageous circumstances of this kind, in which professional obligation was sacrificed in the service of public notoriety, was the appearance of Florida Attorney General Pam Bondi on national television. The Attorney General of the State of Florida is a statewide-elected Cabinet position. The job is essentially to oversee, as the chief law enforcement officer of the state, all the prosecutions and appeals of criminal defendants on a statewide level, and in all death penalty cases.

The Attorney General, as a Cabinet member, is one of the people who might ultimately sit on a Clemency Board considering any person seeking pardons from past criminal prosecutions. As such, the person in this position is often called upon to render legal opinions on questions of law presented to them by law enforcement agencies and other governmental agencies. They hold one of the highest offices of power in the state, and are supposed to be educated, professional and restrained to the utmost degree.

Ms. Bondi apparently forgot these principles and the basis of her office and power when she appeared on national television. In her broadcast appearance, she stated her opinion that Casey Anthony was guilty, and that the evidence against her was overwhelming. The Attorney General had, of course, never met Casey, nor had she spoken with the defense team or even attended any court proceedings. She was totally uninvolved, except as holding the title of Attorney General. But that didn't matter to her. As a politician—and a right-wing Tea Party one at that—she wanted to take advantage of the free publicity; and the fact that a woman's life was at stake did not seem to occur to her.

Now, the Rules of Professional Conduct of the Florida Bar, as well as the Standards of the American Bar Association, prohibit lawyers from making comments about ongoing litigation that they reasonably believe will be disseminated to the public and may impact the outcome of the proceedings. This stricture applies to every lawyer. In 1991, the United States Supreme Court ruled in the case of *Gentile v. State Bar of Nevada* that the right of lawyers to exercise free speech under the First Amendment has to give way in these circumstances to the Sixth Amendment right of counsel and the concept of due process of law. Disgusted by what I saw and heard, I sent Ms. Bondi a letter reminding her of her responsibilities of professional conduct, and pointing out her outrageous misconduct in making such statements publicly. I reproduce the letter as follows.

J. Cheney Mason, P.A.
Attorney and Counsellor at Law

* CRIMINAL LAW
FAMILY LAW
TRIAL PRACTICE-GENERAL

* FLORIDA BAR BOARD CERTIFIED
* NATIONAL BOARD OF TRIAL ADVOCACY CERTIFIED

390 NORTH ORANGE AVENUE, SUITE 2100
ORLANDO, FLORIDA 32801
TELEPHONE (407) 843-5785
FAX (407) 422-6858

April 21, 2011

Pam Bondi, Esq.
Office of the Attorney General
State of Florida
The Capitol PL-01
Tallahassee, Florida 32399

Dear Ms. Bondi:

I am one of the lawyers representing Casey Anthony. I am writing to direct your attention to the Rules of Professional Conduct of the Florida Bar, 4-3.6.

I was amazed to see you participating in the 48 Hours presentation which aired on April 16, 2011. You are supposed to be "the Attorney General" and, thus, the Chief Law Enforcement Officer for the State of Florida. You have no business, whatsoever, involving yourself in any particular case, most especially one that may at some point result in Appeals that your office would be in charge of.

I recognize you apparently were one of the "talking heads" in the early parts of this litigation, before you were an elected official.

Your conduct is reprehensible, unethical, and grossly unprofessional.

I am writing this letter to give you the opportunity to publicly apologize to Ms. Anthony for the outrageous statements you made in that show, and to publicly retract all of your comments.

Not only are your comments memorialized, they are incompetent. You have never met or talked to Casey Anthony; you do not know what the evidence is. You, as Attorney General, are required to comply with the Florida Rules of Professional Conduct. Your actions have eminently threatened the Constitutional Rights of Ms. Anthony and, frankly, have insulted your office.

I will await your response and position anxiously.

Sincerely,

J. Cheney Mason

JCM/kdm
cc: Jose A. Baez, Esq.

One might think that a person holding such an esteemed political position would at least have the professional courtesy to respond to such a letter; as of this very day, even after Casey Anthony's acquittal, Ms. Bondi has never had the integrity or professionalism to respond.

From the beginning of our case, news reporters had acted as prosecutors; but as it went on, the media's efforts to make themselves an actual party to the litigation deepened. Their continued demand for documents and discovery often struck one as an effort of this kind. The information that they allegedly obtained by public record included a daily itinerary of who visited Casey, what she ate and what she bought from the commissary. If any of the defense team met with Casey, this was immediately reported to the media, and when we would arrange for a potential expert witness to meet with Casey, they would rush to publish the witness's name and credentials, along with wild speculations as to what their participation might imply for the strategy of the defense.

Objections to these revelations, and to their intentional impact on the due-process rights of Casey Anthony, fell on deaf ears in the court. Judge Perry claimed that he didn't have the authority to advise or restrict the conduct of the jail in any capacity because of the "Separation of Powers Doctrine." This is a fairly weak argument, since judges order sheriffs to do or not to do things all the time; nevertheless, as usual, our objections failed.

When we would go to visit Casey in jail, we would have to wait for protective security to clear the room from any other visitors, inmates, lawyers or corrections people before Casey could be brought in. Ostensibly this was for her protection. She and we accepted that, and frankly appreciated that special efforts were being taken to protect her from the potential threat of other inmates. The problem, though, was that under these circumstances, we had to meet with her in a large room that was constantly monitored by videotape, which meant we had to be concerned about a new form of unlawful eaves-dropping on our attorney-client confidences.

I had received a confidential tip to be concerned about lip-reading in visitations with Casey, because this was an unusual case. I would be glad I heeded it. I was later given reliable information from a major news network that indeed they had employed professional lip-readers to try to decipher what was being said in confidence. Every time we had to approach the bench for "sidebar conferences," I was mindful of the cameras focused on me and kept a hand in front of my mouth as much as possible. On a few occasions I was reminded that the court reporter was unable to hear what I was saying. Often this advice came from Mr. Ashton; though I have no way of knowing whether the prosecution was aware of the presence of lip-readers in court, he usually kept his own back to all of the cameras, putting the focus of any such interlopers squarely on Mr. Baez and myself.

We filed several motions and had hearings with the court, attempting to rein in such media interference with the trial, but were denied on each front. An instance of this sort of over-involvement that many of my lawyer friends around the country simply had a hard time believing was the media's spying on the defense proceedings.

Throughout the pretrial proceedings the media would be given priority seating in the courtroom audience, right behind the defense table, where they would do their best to eavesdrop on our conversations. The courtrooms were already wired with sensitive microphones, which were on all the time. Anything you said at the defense table was recorded and made available to the media, unless you remembered to push and hold the button down to disconnect the microphone. Yet this information was hardly enough for our media eavesdroppers. On one occasion I realized that a television camera positioned on a high tripod was able to look over my shoulder and view notes between

Casey and me. On another, while I was at the counsel table studying a copy of an appellate court decision, a cameraman used a telephoto lens to zoom in on what I was reading and photograph it for publication.

When it came time to set the stage for the trial, I insisted on relocating the defense table over to the side of the courtroom where no media could be behind us, and all the telephoto lenses could see would be our faces or the backs of our computer screens. Judge Perry graciously accommodated us in this regard, and the reconfiguration of the courtroom was completed before we left to conduct our out-of-town jury selection.

Unfortunately, when we relocated to Clearwater for the selection process, we found that the courtroom there was configured differently. Again the news media were allowed to position themselves and their cameras so as to be able to eavesdrop in on our conversations and notes. We had to develop a coded system in order to make it impossible for them to get any real meaning out of what they saw.

Furthermore, the configuration of the trial courtroom, which we thought would give us an advantage against the media's spying, proved to be a problem in a different and unpredicted way. By being placed where we were, we afforded the judge the opportunity to hear what we were saying during breaks and recesses. He would stand behind us by the doorway on some of the occasions during which Casey and I had private conversations at the counsel table, and was even able to overhear our voices from the holding cell when Casey conferred with the other lawyers and me. It had never occurred to us that he could or would listen in on us in such a way, or that, having once heard us, he would not simply block it out of his mind or warn us on subsequent occasions to keep our voices down. Yet as will be discussed toward the end of this book, the judge would have a few surprises in store for us in this regard.

10

Talkers and Walkers

Many high-profile cases today seem to overflow with lawyers anxious to be seen on TV. One might think that a person who has gone through seven years of college to obtain a Juris Doctorate degree, then passed the bar exam to become a lawyer, would have more discretion than to outwardly exhibit such attention-seeking motives, even if they couldn't help feeling them; but apparently they no longer do.

I should be clear that I am not arguing categorically against lawyer publicity. There are certainly situations in which it is not only appropriate, but necessary in balancing the turmoil surrounding a case, for a lawyer involved in that case to make public statements. What I'm more concerned about are the "big talkers" who volunteer to comment on or analyze cases with which they have no official contact or involvement. Casey Anthony's trial, by nature of its enormous media presence, became an epicenter of such egregious conduct. Lawyer after lawyer lined up to be interviewed, even to the point of repeatedly soliciting the opportunity to do so themselves. It's easy to discount this type of behavior by relegating it to economic motivations, and in many cases lawyers do in fact believe that having their faces on TV will increase their chances of being sought out, hired and offered more money for their services. In some cases, perhaps, it's even true. More often than not, however, it has surprisingly little to do with economic reasons, and more to do with the personality of the lawyers in question.

In the "Case Against Casey" the news media, pressed hourly and nightly to boost their ratings with new information about the case, were constantly on the lookout for people to fill in the gaps between actual occurrences. When lawyers were contacted for commentary or analysis, most of them soon realized that they needed to salt whatever story they had to tell with inflammatory comments in order to give the journalists what they wanted. In the end, a number of lawyers gave in to this pressure and claimed to have a greater depth of experience and relevant knowledge than they had. They showed no hesitation in ventilating unqualified opinions about "what was going to happen" or "what should happen," very often discoursing at length on what *they* would do if they were on the case, and what the defense lawyers were doing wrong.

Many of these big talkers, unsatisfied with pronouncing on the case from a distance, tried to involve themselves in a more direct capacity. One tried repeatedly to have himself drafted onto the defense team, both before and after criticizing our strategies—and despite never having been involved in a similar case before. Another, who had had some law experience but no major experience with criminal cases, confronted me directly on two occasions, telling me I "really needed" his help. I would have loved to be a fly on the wall when *he* heard the verdict.

Fortunately, I had had the opportunity sometime before the trial to recommend a few lawyers to the media who had actually "been in the trenches" and were qualified to make legitimate commentary, several of whom were in fact contacted and contributed very reasonable analyses as to the proceedings. Not surprisingly, however, these lawyers did not garner as much limelight as those with more sensationalistic predilections.

Complementing the ubiquity of these big talkers was the astonishing level of attrition on the side of the defense. On the one hand it was difficult to find lawyers willing to work for free, and on behalf of so controversial a client; on the other, alongside and sometimes underlying the eagerness of those who did join the defense were other motives, some of them questionable ones, that took valuable time to uncover. The case seemed simultaneously to attract and repel participants, and we were often left to speculate on the reasons we had been left in the lurch.

Among our last-minute losses were a number of major forensic experts, including the renowned criminologist Henry Lee. Dr. Lee, you will recall, had been involved in the case early on and had provided us with a great deal of valuable information regarding Caylee's remains, her clothing and the various crime scenes under investigation. Chief among his contributions were arguments against the numerous fallacies and shortcomings of the State's forensic case, which I had expected Dr. Lee to present in person during the trial. Unfortunately, however, when that time came, he backed out. Apparently he had recently begun a forensic training school that would be attended almost exclusively by law enforcement personnel from around the country, and had been experiencing a great deal of pressure to withdraw—whether real or imaginary, I could not determine—from his intended student body.

Expert trial consultants were no more reliable. Having been denied reimbursement from the Justice Administrative Commission for a jury consulting expert—on the supposed basis of my expertise in such matters—we were left to seek the assistance of such an expert on our own. One fellow in California agreed to help us, then bailed out on us about two weeks before trial time. I never did get a clear reason from him as to why.

By this point our plans relied heavily on his input, so I immediately reached out to two well-known and reliable jury consulting experts, Sandy Marks from Miami and Bob Hirschhorn from Houston. Both had prior commitments that would not allow them to attend the trial, but both were willing to help and very graciously sent us some helpful questioning suggestions in the form of jury questionnaires. Hoping to utilize these in our jury selection process, I filed the following motion with the court.

**IN THE CIRCUIT COURT FOR THE NINTH JUDICIAL CIRCUIT
IN AND FOR ORANGE COUNTY, FLORIDA**

STATE OF FLORIDA,   CASE NO.: 482008-CF-0015606-O
      Plaintiff,   Judge Perry

vs.

CASEY MARIE ANTHONY,
      Defendant.
_____/

AMENDED MOTION TO UTILIZE JUROR QUESTIONNAIRE

COMES NOW the Defendant, CASEY ANTHONY, by and through her undersigned

counsel, and pursuant to Fla. R. Crim. P 3.281, the Fifth, Sixth, Eighth, and Fourteenth

Amendments to the United States Constitution, Article I, sections 2, 9, 16, 17, 21, and 22 of the

Florida Constitution, hereby files and furnishes and serves upon this Court and all parties hereto

of her Amended Motion to Utilize Juror Questionnaire in order to expedite the jury selection

process in in support asserts the following:

1. A capital case presents diverse and unique issues that must be addressed during *voir dire*.

    The use of a questionnaire is authorized and anticipated for complex criminal cases under

    Fla. R. Crim. P. 3.281. Along with the list of the names and addresses of prospective

    jurors that have been summoned to try the case, the undersigned is entitled to receive

    "copies of all jury questionnaires returned by the prospective jurors." Form 1.984 sets

    forth a standard jury questionnaire for civil cases. Although there is no standard

    questionnaire for criminal cases, the use of jury questionnaires in serious criminal cases is

    commonplace. *(See Windom v. State*, 656 So. 2d 432 (Fla. 1995), cert. denied, 516 U.S.

    1012 (1995); (capital case); *Esty v. State*, 642 So. 2d 1074 (Fla. 1994) (capital case);

    Kramer v. State, 619 So. 2d 274 (Fla. 1993) (capital case); *Mansell v. State*, 609 So. 2d

679 (Fla. 1st DCA 1992) (trafficking in cocaine case); *See* Fla. R. Crim. P. 3.281).

Indeed, in capital cases "experienced capital defenders do not use standard form

questionnaires; each capital defendant, each capital case, and each local jury pool are so

distinct that they require highly individualized surveys." Blume, Johnston, and

Threlkeld, *"Probing Life Qualification Through Expanded Voir Dire"*, 29 HOFSTRA L.

REV. 1209, 1255 (2001).

2. Judges, lawyers, and commentators across the United States have acknowledged the

   value of questionnaires, and have frequently endorsed using them. *See*, e.g., *United*

   States v. Layton, 632 F. Supp. 176, 177 (N.D. Cal 1986). This is so because "preliminary

   questionnaires promise both time – savings and increased candor." *See*, Blume, et. al,

   supra, at 1254. Inasmuch as "jurors are willing to admit unfavorable opinions in written

   responses to questionnaires that they would hesitate to review out loud....," *See*

   "Choosing the Best Jurors and Establishing a Theme of the Case," 13 Crim. Prac. Rep

   316 (1999), and that "each capital case...require[s] highly individualized surveys,"

   Blume, et.al, supra, the Court should welcome the idea of a questionnaire.

3. As stated by the Supreme Court with respect to capital jury selection, because of "the

   range of discretion entrusted to a jury in a capital sentencing hearing, there is a unique

   opportunity for...prejudice to operate but remain undetected." *Turner v. Murray*, 476

   U.S. 28, 35 (1986) (plurality). This risk, said the high court, "is especially serious in light

   of the complete finality of the death sentence." *Id.*

4. Indeed, given the fact that in capital cases, like this one, heightened standards of due

   process apply, *See Mills v. Maryland*, 486 U.S. 367 (1988), *Elledge v. State*, 346 So. 2d

998 (Fla. 1977), it is all the more important that the Court be absolutely convinced that the jury selected is fair and impartial.

5. As stated by this Court, this case is different. The unprecedented, primarily negative media coverage; the hostility toward the general public toward the Defendant; and the unique issues related to all capital cases requires a jury questionnaire. Such a questionnaire would allow a thorough and necessary exploration of jurors' predisposition, thus eliminating the potential of a partiality while also reducing the time required for individual voir dire.

6. Under these circumstances, a jury questionnaire on at least three critical issues – pretrial publicity, the hostility of the general public toward the defendant, and the death penalty – is not only warranted, but necessary to obtain the most candid responses and to ensure a fair and impartial jury. In light of the time that has been consumed in the process, the defense respectfully requests that this Honorable Court allow the use of juror questionnaires for potential jurors while those jurors are waiting for individual voir dire. The use of questionnaires will make product use of the potential jurors' time and allow a full and candid exploration of jurors' ability to be fair and impartial.

This space intentionally left blank

Following the State's objection, Judge Perry denied this motion, forcing us to reach out yet again, this time to a woman known for her jury-consultation credentials. Having initially agreed to participate, this expert too backed out, supposedly due to a medical condition. Yet despite the fact that she had had nothing to do with our jury selection or the case in general, she went on a speaking circuit after the trial was done, claiming to have played an instrumental jury-consultation role in Casey Anthony's defense—a behavior we would come to find all too common.

Two of the lawyers that were brought onto the defense team early on had books out—not concerning this case, but others—and both of them used their appearances on national TV primarily to hawk their books. At trial time, again, neither was anywhere to be found. Upon their disappearance, I made the decision to seek a female lawyer to fill the vacant role of death-penalty counsel, as it had been a woman who had occupied it previously. I reached out to five female lawyers that I knew around the country—each a former president of the National Association of Criminal Defense Lawyers, and each highly qualified to assist us. Unfortunately, as it turned out, each had justifiable and understandable reasons they could not assist, including conflicts with other cases and economic limitations.

One of my colleagues, a senior judge, suggested another experienced female attorney known to me, whom I had overlooked in my list. We contacted her and recruited her to the team, and initially, she was very helpful; after the jury selection had been completed, and for reasons still unknown, she disappeared from the trial for all but one or two days, only reappearing after the successful verdict. It was hard to view her reappearance without suspicion; but this was exactly the sort of occurrence that, amid all of the case's attendant hardships and temptations, plagued the defense of Casey Anthony throughout. It would seem almost sheer luck that brought together the team as it stood at trial time.

For many years the Florida Association of Criminal Defense Lawyers has sponsored a dedicated seminar on death-penalty issues. This program, known as "Death Is Different," features a number of speakers with experience in various fields of defense, as well as experts on particular matters that may affect the proper defense of a death-penalty case. Mr. Baez, though courageous and energetic, was short on experience with homicide and death-penalty cases and was anxious to go.

We arrived at the seminar during a portion of a presentation by a woman named Dorothy Clay Sims. Ms. Sims is not a criminal defense lawyer, but rather a lawyer who specializes in preparing other attorneys to cross-examine medical experts; and in this field is well established throughout the country. At the time I had not heard of Ms. Sims before, but I was immediately impressed by her presence and demeanor. She was substantially different from many of the speakers that the seminar had had over the years, who generally tried to appear otherwise than as sophisticated and well-dressed lawyers. She was impeccably dressed and groomed, with a highly professional posture; yet while she showed herself to be serious and committed, she retained a winning sense of humor. With these qualities she had already established a wide network of researchers to assist her, and she brought substantial computer skills to boot. I knew she was the woman we had been looking for.

Ms. Sims's seminar presentation was commanding. She expressed her personal and emotional convictions in opposition to the death penalty, then went on to advise different methods of preparation for the cross-examination of experts. After her presentation I approached her, and after a formal introduction—she had recognized us initially from all the news coverage of the case—asked her bluntly if she would consider joining our team. I was surprised when she responded with an enthusiastic "yes." At that point I confessed to her that we had no money, and that if she joined us, it would have to be on a pro-bono basis. I wrote this on the back of my business card and handed it to her, upon which she flashed an ear-to-ear smile and immediately agreed.

Traditionally the primary speaker at these same "Death Is Different" seminars had been Judge O.H. Eaton, Jr., a highly respected figure in the legal world who was now winding up his judicial career. Judge Eaton, best known as the author of the death-penalty law "Bible," is relied upon by the Judicial Conference and judges around the country as an authority in all matters dealing with the law and the death penalty, and had been a friend and colleague of mine long before attaining to the bench.

Coincidentally, some time before the conference where we met Dorothy Sims, Judge Eaton had been responsible for another valuable addition to Casey Anthony's defense. He had suggested that I acquire an intern for our team, and recommended a young law student who had been working for him in the Eighteenth Judicial Circuit. Lis Fryer, he had told me, had done a remarkable job as an intern for the judges in Seminole County. Her research and writing skills were excellent, and her high work ethic far beyond that of the average or even above-average law student; but her term of internship with him was expiring, and she needed placement somewhere to finish her educational requirements.

By that time I had been practicing for around forty years without an intern, but I saw the sense of Judge Eaton's suggestion immediately. Particularly in situations like Casey's, a solid intern would be an invaluable—and economic—addition to the team; so I called Lis Fryer and arranged an interview.

My first impression of Lis was that she couldn't possibly be old enough to be doing this. As Dorothy would later describe her, she looked like a high-school senior. She had a clear, cherubic face, short, brown hair, and a smile and energy that only comes with youth. Her looks were deceiving, however;

it turned out that she had been married for a long time and had a seventeen-year-old son and a seven-year-old daughter. Though a new lawyer, she was evidently mature far beyond her years.

On the basis of this interview, and the strength of Judge Eaton's recommendation, I brought Lis onto the team. I knew right away that it had been the right decision. She met Judge Eaton's endorsements completely and immediately began working tirelessly on every project and research issue I threw at her. Yet there were other qualities that made her a crucial participant in this particular case. To begin with, she was philosophically and politically committed against the death penalty, and she had not been biased against Casey Anthony by the news because, as it turned out, she didn't have a television—a fact that was also true of Dorothy.

With these two remarkable women on our team, it seemed to me as though the stars were lining up. On more than one occasion I told Mr. Baez that though I believed that at the end of the day there would be few left standing, I was certain he could count on Dorothy, Lis and me; this would prove almost literally true. In the end, the only ones left were the three of us, Mr. Baez and some very hard working interns and associates that he had brought onto the case, two of whom I feel I should name here in gratitude. Michelle Medina and Will Slabaugh were hard working and utterly reliable, and made an indispensable part of our team.

With such a dedicated, selfless group on our side, none of whom were remotely interested in publicity or financial gain, I could not but draw the dramatic comparison between them and the talking-head lawyers scrambling for the attention of the news. These lawyers would take occasion to speak publicly about anything and everything they could—even parts of the case they knew absolutely nothing about—in order to arrogate a fictitious expertise to themselves. They pandered shamelessly to the media narrative they were brought in to corroborate and never allowed humility or reasonable self-doubt to hold them back for a moment from their enthusiastic pursuit of notoriety.

Yet in the end, the big talkers lost to the real walkers—the hard workers that will go on to great careers. I expect Lis Fryer will reach the Supreme Court one day, if she chooses to. Dorothy will continue in her illustrious career, greatly respected by all who deal with her. Michelle and Will, our young lawyers, will earn their stripes by continuing to work as hard as they did for us. The media puppets, eager as they are for public attention, will remain exactly that.

11

The Noise Before the Storm

In Florida, all State Court criminal cases are essentially managed by the Florida Rules of Criminal Procedure. These are rules that originate, for the most part, in the Rules Committee of the Florida Bar Association and are laid out by the Supreme Court for utilization in the processes of every criminal case under state law.

Perhaps the most critical of these rules are the ones related to what we have already referred to as "discovery." These discovery rules govern the ability of both sides of a criminal case to learn as much about the case as possible, by providing for the production of documents and the identification of witnesses well in advance of a trial. The overall goal is to prevent surprises during trial, or as we call them, "trials by ambush."

In Florida, there has been much debate over the years about this discovery process. Predictably, such stalwart constitutionalists as the Florida Sheriff's Association and the Prosecuting Attorneys Association have wanted to eliminate the process altogether; after all, it very frequently helps defendants. Consistent statistics show that over ninety-four percent of the criminal cases in Florida are resolved through plea bargains, which almost always arise from open discovery. Frequently, prosecutors as well as defense lawyers learn that the evidence at hand is not quite what the police have claimed, and cases are dismissed. Justice is often served very sufficiently in this manner, and the fiscal savings to the taxpayer is huge—to say nothing of the avoidance of wasted time and energy. If every case had to go through the whole process of a jury trial, there would simply not be enough judges, prosecutors, defense lawyers, courthouses and courtrooms to handle them all.

In order to get Casey Anthony's case to trial on a tight schedule, Judge Perry entered a special order requiring certain things to be done within certain time frames. This order was not based upon the well-established Florida discovery procedures, but determined by the judge, and arguably within his discretion. One of its requirements was that all expert witnesses either provide a report of their intended testimony along with their background, or agree to sit for depositions, or not be allowed to testify.

The defense is not required to engage in the discovery process; for that side, discovery is optional. Yet the intent to participate in discovery is the rule rather than the exception and is invoked by defendants in the overwhelming majority of cases in which defendants lack the resources to engage in discovery without the State and proceed with their own investigation. When the defendant initiates the process of mutual discovery by demanding discovery from the prosecution, the prosecution is required to provide the defense with their full witness list and all documents and records relevant to the case within fifteen days.

In our case, they were still providing discovery information to us three years later, and even during the trial itself. Those bent on a justice system skewed, as ours is, to the benefit of the prosecution, argue that the request represents a continuing duty to disclose, no matter when it is carried out. It is reasonable to think this in a general sense, but in our case it seemed somewhat incredible that huge amounts of discovery would only be available and revealed one, two and three years into the process. Along with other circumstances in the conduct of the prosecution, it reinforced the continuing pattern of obstructionist behavior that we have been discussing. This brings us to one of the major skirmishes that occurred in what I thought of as "the noise before the storm."

In the middle of November 2010, well into the process, Mr. Ashton filed a paper entitled "Motion to Compel Additional Discovery." In this motion, relevant to the deposition of expert witnesses, he requested the production of:

1. Any contracts or agreements in any manner or form setting forth the scope of work or expected compensation.
2. Any communications between the expert and any member of the defense team, either past or present, or any member of their staff, or anyone working on behalf of the defendant.
3. All records or bills submitted by or payments made to the expert.
4. All records pertaining to payments for travel, meals or entertainment paid to or for the benefit of the expert or anyone traveling with the expert by any member of the defense team either past or present or any member of their staff or anyone working on behalf of the defendant.
5. Any notes taken by the expert or for the expert during or referencing their examination of any evidence in this case.
6. Any photograph or video taken by the expert in connection with this case.

These requests were absurd for a number of reasons. To begin with, recall that all of the work being done in this case was being done pro bono or, on the finding of the defendant's indigency, under expenses paid by the State. Since Mr. Ashton knew full well that Casey had been declared indigent, and that all expenses related to experts and similar defense preparation were paid through the Justice Administrative Commission, if at all, for him to request records pertaining to expert expenses was redundant at best, and at worst, a pernicious attempt to waste the defense's time.

The request for notes or communications between any member of the defense and experts was equally questionable. There is a privilege known throughout the law, everywhere in the United States, according to which attorney *work product* information is not discoverable. Communications and notes between experts and members of the defense team fall squarely into that category—again, something that Mr. Ashton knew very well.

Refreshingly, the court agreed with us. The judge denied the requests in paragraphs 1, 2, 3 and 4, in essence telling the State to take the depositions of its witnesses in the usual process. He did essentially grant Mr. Ashton's motion as to paragraphs 5 and 6, however, excepting any part that would be deemed "work product."

The provisions in his order that started the whole deterioration of the process were in a section of it that read, "…and Defendant shall also provide to the State a list of Defendant's experts that shall include the subject matter as to what the experts will testify to and the area of expertise for each expert." It would seem that this would be a simple matter: give the State the names of all experts and their relevant subject matter. But though the plain language of that order was complied with by the defense, it was not sufficient for the prosecution. What they really wanted was to require the defense to tell them everything that a witness might have to say, revealing all of our strategies and theories in advance; in the general obstructionist course of the "Case Against Casey," they would use these simple strictures not only to obtain more information than they were entitled to by due process, but to harass the defense in strange and petty ways.

Following the proceedings as described, but before any paperwork was officially filed by the court, a series of e-mails were exchanged between Mr. Baez and Mr. Ashton regarding the court's pronouncements. First was Mr. Baez's e-mail to Prosecutor Ashton listing the names of our experts, their specific fields of expertise and their addresses. He also invited Mr. Ashton to advise him if there were any additional matters he needed to know—specifically, any questions regarding these experts.

Mr. Ashton's response was simply that he didn't think Mr. Baez's list was in compliance with the court's order, which had required the defense to include, in this list, subject matter "as to what the experts will testify to and their area of expertise."

Mr. Baez responded, again providing a detailed list of names, along with fields of expertise, addresses and what each expert would testify about. As these testimonies had not yet taken place, he could hardly have said more about them; but this was not enough for the prosecution. In Mr. Ashton's next response he pushed for still more information, demanding "a written statement of the substance of their testimony as ordered by the court." It had not been the *substance*, but the *subject matter*, of the experts' testimony that had been required by the court's ruling. Mr. Baez, realizing that the prosecution was trying to harass him, dug in and insisted on this point, referring to the specific wording of the order.

Ultimately, a hearing had to be scheduled to settle what the court had meant by "subject matter." In this hearing, Judge Perry entered an order stating that his original order had in fact required more information than what Mr. Baez had already provided to the prosecution. Ordered to provide more, the defense team first attempted to fax the information, some three hundred pages of documents. This was refused by the Clerk of Court, who claimed it was too great a volume; yet at that time the court was not capable of receiving information electronically either, so one of our young lawyers, Will Slabaugh, had to make a mad dash to copy all of the documents and hand-deliver them to Orlando. Arriving two minutes after closing time, and finding himself barred both from the courthouse and from the neighboring State Attorney's Office—where people were still working—he delivered the papers first thing the following morning. Again, however, this was not enough for the prosecution—now living up to its name in more ways than the strictly professional—and Judge Perry, in compliance with sanctions sought by Mr. Ashton for contempt of court, assessed costs against Mr. Baez in the amount of almost six hundred dollars.

In an effort to exonerate Mr. Baez from the sanctions imposed by the court, the defense submitted a "Motion for Reconsideration," in which were outlined not only an explanation of the foregoing debacle, but also the names and as much specific detail as could possibly be provided with respect to each of our witnesses. One might have thought there would be nothing left to complain about—but the Motion was rejected in full, and the sanctions remained in place.

It might be pointed out here, lest there be any suspicion of fairness in my presentation of the facts, that later in trial, when it was disclosed that the State had failed to reveal to the defense the "evidence" of the morphed video that they were allowed to use in trial, there was no corresponding sanction against Mr. Ashton. Nor, when sealed testimonies from a psychiatrist who had evaluated Casey Anthony were admittedly opened by the prosecution, and their contents related to George and Cindy Anthony *despite the express order of the court*, were any such reprimands effected.

And as if this weren't sufficient evidence of court bias, the judge further ordered, in upholding sanctions against Mr. Baez, that any opinions not expressed in written reports or through deposition would not be allowed in trial. This essentially amounted to an invitation to the State to strategically obstruct the defendant's rights: unless the defense were somehow able to predict everything that an expert witness might say directly or during cross-examination, and write it down beforehand, all Mr. Ashton had to do was strategically fail to take their deposition—a voluntary choice on his part—and then ask the judge to reject their testimony on the grounds that his order hadn't been complied with. In any criminal case in the United States, and particularly in a capital case, to give the prosecution so unchecked an ability to prevent the presentation of complete testimony to a jury is absolutely outrageous; yet our objections to this measure were struck down also.

The media had, of course, been involved with our case from the beginning, but the degree to which even our second judge considered it a partner to the proceedings was often baffling. Nothing seemed to lie outside its purview, which led to some further "noises before the storm."

Under Florida law, if Casey Anthony were ultimately convicted of first-degree murder, and the State wished to put her to death for it, there would be a secondary trial known as the "penalty phase," a proceeding in which the defense has the opportunity to present witnesses and evidence in favor of the defendant in hopes of averting the death penalty. Whether or not to impose this penalty is the most difficult and somber decision a court can make, so regardless how the decision falls, the importance of this phase is undisputable.

In Casey Anthony's case, the defense, recognizing the potential for a penalty phase, wished to seal the matters that might prove relevant in such a phase, such that they would not be disclosed to the world in advance of a trial. We intended to pursue—and fully anticipated—an acquittal; but we had to plan for the worst, and wanted in that case to have our side heard without the prejudice and misinformation that had plagued it thus far.

Pursuant to these wishes, Judge Perry set up a penalty phase hearing in advance to settle whether or not the information in question would be sealed; yet in doing so, he ordered that the defense counsel provide notice of the motion and hearing "...to all interested persons and entities, **including the media.**" This made it clear, to anyone who was still in the dark about it, that Judge Perry considered the media a party to the litigation. It was precisely the media's involvement in these matters that we hoped to curtail, but the judge's condition for even *considering* that option was that we allow the media to be present at our discussion of them! Fortunately, Casey's trial did not require a penalty phase, so it never went any further than this; but if she *had* been convicted, nothing that could be said in her defense could have been presented prior to its full exposure to—and subsequent distortion by—the media machine.

Another big difficulty, also directly related to media malfeasance, revolved around the issue of where the trial itself would take place.

Sometimes, as in Casey Anthony's trial, the notoriety of a particular case reaches such a level that it is unlikely, or at least unreasonable to expect, that one will be able to impanel a fair jury in a given jurisdiction, and another location has to be selected in which to conduct the trial. Our history reveals numerous significant instances of this. I recall one several years ago that involved charges against police officers in Miami, in which the media saturation around that case was such that the jury was completely stacked against the defendants ahead of time. One of the best lawyers in the country defended the case and attempted to get a change of venue granted. This was denied, and he lost the case. Upon conviction he appealed, and the Supreme Court—specifically referring to the trial atmosphere created by the media as being like a "circus"—granted a new trial in a new venue. In their new trial, the defendants were all acquitted.

Media ubiquity notwithstanding, however, a change of venue is still a somewhat rare and exceptional proceeding. Efforts must first be made to select a jury local to the area in which a crime occurred; even in the rare case of a move, neither the State nor the defense can simply pick other places where they want the case to be tried. In another capital murder case I tried a few years before Casey's, repeated efforts to change the venue were denied, and only after a very lengthy process—involving the individual questioning of around 635 prospective jurors—was a jury selected. Interestingly, we were also denied our requests to have the jury sequestered in that case—a request that seems increasingly essential to jury objectivity, given the intrusiveness of the media in our time.

In our case, the judge agreed pretrial that this was one of those exceptional situations that called for a move. Casey Anthony's case had already been subjected to such intense media scrutiny that a fair trial would be unlikely in Orange County; so rather than go through the time and expense of selecting a local jury, and then have to make arrangements to take the show out of town, the judge agreed to relocate the trial in advance.

In such a case, the judge contacts a chief judge in another circuit to make arrangements to move the trial there. It goes without saying that the location cannot be just anywhere. The rules of relocation, resulting from numerous appellate court decisions, include that the site to which the trial is to be moved

must be as demographically similar as possible to where the case was originally to be held; so Judge Perry had to look at statistical information provided
by defense research, along with information presumably given by the prosecution, in order to find other areas in Florida that would be demographically
similar to Orlando. Once he had decided on a location, he kept it to himself.

Now, secrecy in such a matter is not unusual, but in this case it fell into
the same bias in favor of the prosecution that the rest of the case was already
following, for much the same reason. Remember, the prosecution in this case
had unlimited financial and investigative resources to bring to bear on the
case, while the defense had nothing other than the resolve and imagination
of our pro bono lawyers and whatever the JAC would allow us to spend for
investigative and other miscellaneous costs. In such a situation, it would arguably have been fairer for the judge to have provided everyone with the new
location as soon as he had made his arrangements, at which point the defense
could have begun an investigation, at least in some capacity, into the new de-
mographic and solicited volunteer cooperation from other defense lawyers
in the area. Yet we found out virtually at the last minute—a mere five days in
advance of the move—and that only after repeated requests.

The new location was to be Clearwater, in Pinellas County, on the west
coast of Florida. It was crucial that this new location not be publicized, and
all of the lawyers on the case were forbidden, under charge of contempt, from
revealing to anyone where we were going. This meant, of course, that we could
not even make hotel reservations in advance under my name or Mr. Baez's,
so the defense had to arrange for hotel rooms using my wife's maiden name.
It also meant that Mr. Baez and I had to stay in separate places—for our own
safety.

The process of picking the jury was likely to be lengthy and repetitive,
and we would likely only have the evenings for study and review of witness

files and other trial documents. Taking along about eight banker's boxes full of files, along with all of the other essentials for a two- or three-week stay, we moved into the lodgings we were able to reserve in the few days prior to jury selection. With a twenty-four-hour head start on the media, we were able to settle in without being detected and begin planning for the campaign ahead; but the paparazzi were not far behind, and once they knew where we had moved, it was a matter of hours before they had gathered again *en masse*, clamoring around our doorstep.

12

Pick Your Team

A very important bit of knowledge that the citizens of our country do not often have is the understanding of what a grand jury is. The type of jury that tries the cases most of us are used to seeing is called a petit (sometimes pronounced "petty") jury. This usually leads people to believe that the grand jury is simply a bigger and more important version of the same jury. It is indeed bigger, and in some regards more important, since its members bring formal accusations against a defendant; but there are other, much more important legal differences that should be understood.

A grand jury, like a petit jury, is a group of random citizens subpoenaed to appear for that duty. Unlike a petit jury, however, they do not hear or decide trials. They only decide whether there is or is not probable cause to file an indictment, or formal accusation, against someone. In this sense the members of a grand jury rarely do anything on their own. They do what they are directed or requested to do by the prosecuting attorney—and only the prosecuting attorney.

When the grand jury is in session, the prosecutors bring them statements about whatever case they want the grand jury to consider. If the police make an arrest in a case that they believe warrants the death penalty, then under Florida law the accusatorial writ cannot simply be filed by the prosecution, but must be formally "returned" by the grand jury. In this case the prosecuting attorney goes before the grand jury and, usually with one or two law enforcement officers as witnesses, tells them that they are going to hear the case of the State of Florida versus So-and-so, who has been arrested and charged with, say, murder.

Strictly speaking, there are no defense lawyers in grand jury proceedings. A few years ago we were able to convince the legislature to allow them to accompany witnesses, so now they can sit next to witnesses—as long as they don't say anything. In this situation defense lawyers are not allowed to make objections, argue law or make any statements to the grand jury; all they can do is make "congressional whispers" in the ear of their client. Another big difference is that there is no judge before a grand jury. A judge swears in the members of a grand jury after they are statutorily qualified, but that's the last time they'll see one—unless and until they return an indictment.

An indictment is returned by the grand jury solely on the basis of the prosecutor's presentation. The prosecutor is supposed to inform them of the facts, and then corroborate those facts by having witnesses testify; however, there being no one present to gauge the propriety of the witnesses' testimonies, there is a decided bias to such cases. Only the prosecutor is present to conduct witness testimony and to argue in favor of indictment; only the prosecutor is present to tell jurors what the law is in case of any ambiguity.

It may well be argued that the revolutionary concept of a grand jury, which dates back to the creation of this country, has long since lost its usefulness. Originally grand juries were intended to act as a buffer between the king and the people; today, in our present state of government, their principal function is to provide the prosecuting attorney with a validating front to hide behind.

If a person is going to be charged with a crime, as the prosecutor wants, the prosecutor is able simply to tell the press and public that "the grand jury has made a decision," or that "the grand jury brought the indictment"—which gives otherwise uninformed citizens the impression that a formal proceeding has transpired, in relation to which the actual jury trials that we are used to must constitute a kind of official formality.

In our case, with all its media coverage and public prejudgment, this misperception was illustrated over and over again. Whenever Judge Perry would announce that "the *grand jury* sitting in and for Orange County, Florida has returned the indictment," the impression would be produced far and wide that a great decision had been brought to bear—all, of course, in favor of the prosecution. The fact that the general public were told, as always, that they could not accept such an indictment as evidence meant essentially nothing to them, as it does whenever grand jury proceedings are confused with those of other juries.

It has often been said by trial lawyers, professors and knowledgeable observers that trials are won or lost in the process of selecting a jury. I don't necessarily adhere to this opinion entirely, but I do recognize the merit of it, and I can appreciate the paradox that with all the importance attached to the process, there are probably as many opinions of how to properly select a jury as there are lawyers doing it. There is no right or wrong way; but one way or another, the lawyer's personality has to shine through the darkness of uncertainty that necessarily attends an undecided case. If a lawyer does not believe in their client and case, the jury will most certainly pick up on it.

The process itself, formally termed *voir dire*, is supposed to help the participants in a trial, and the court itself, by disqualifying anyone for jury participation who holds preconceived notions, thoughts or base prejudices that may hinder their fair judgment. Lawyers use it, whenever possible, to conduct something of a mini trial; during it we try to learn as much about prospective jurors as possible and hopefully get them to reveal something about themselves that will aid us in deciding to keep or dismiss them.

In all jury selection processes, both sides have what are known as "challenges"—opportunities to tell the judge that they don't accept a particular person as a juror in the case. There are two types of challenges: challenges for cause and peremptory challenges. Challenges for cause are those that are based upon a specific statement or position taken by a potential juror that, on its face, suggests that they are unable to render a fair judgment. This is the case even when a juror displays uncertainty in an answer to a question; in death-penalty cases, a prospective juror who says that he or she could not impose the death penalty, or is unsure about whether they could impose it, is immediately subject to removal on this basis. Peremptory challenges are special challenges, limited in number depending on the type of trial and the jurisdiction, that we lawyers can make simply on the basis of personal feeling. This may have to do with a prospective juror's body language, the way they speak, or many other human traits. Naturally there are exceptions to the qualities open to peremptory challenge, including racial and gender minority membership.

It is common that a prospective juror who appears "on paper" to be a proper candidate for a particular jury is revealed by questioning to have aspects of his or her personality, philosophy, politics, religion and the like that disqualify him or her from it altogether. Accordingly, though prospective jurors are often told, by lawyers and judges alike, that a questioning lawyer is not attempting to pry into their lives, nothing could be further from the truth. Any and every detail might provide insight into a person's character, and a good lawyer will try to find out as much as he can.

In order to save time—and, hopefully, any embarrassment to the prospective juror—lawyers frequently use jury questionnaires. These are series of written questions that prospective jurors can answer privately, which allows for, among other things, a tactful assessment of such potentially sensitive characteristics as education level and membership in certain organizations. As I mentioned in a previous chapter, we had jury questionnaires submitted to us by a pair of well-qualified jury-consultation experts, neither of whom was able to attend the trial itself. Their questionnaires would have been absolutely beneficial and time saving, but the judge would not allow them, because the State had objected. Why? The simple answer is that an overwhelming public prejudice had already been created and reaffirmed over and over again by the media; in light of which, the prosecutors knew that the odds were greatly in favor of their finding jurors who had already made up their minds against Casey—and they wanted to keep it that way.

Before the selection process began, Judge Perry had promised the members of the news media—in response to the demands of TV producers trying to anticipate their coverage budgets—that it would be completed in five days. When I learned that he had told them this, I was appalled. I had tried a number of similar cases, though none as high profile as this one, and knew that a jury could not be picked out for a case like this in that amount of time. In my estimate, which I discussed with the judge, it would take between two and three weeks; and this turned out to be pretty close to the truth. (It ended up taking the work-hour equivalent of three weeks of court time.)

On the first day of jury selection, the courthouse in Clearwater had helicopters hovering overhead and a virtual convoy of news trucks converging on it. Crowds of curiosity-seekers flocked to the scene, many of them still unaware of the nature of the circus that had suddenly appeared in town. Hundreds of people were subpoenaed to jury duty, and though cases are to be kept confidential during the jury-selection process, it didn't take long for them to infer from the media storm outside the courthouse what case they were being called to.

The courtroom assigned was a large one, with an aura of great but somewhat oppressive importance. Unlike the prosecution, which had the entire attached State Attorney's Office at its disposal, the defense didn't have an office on site, so the court administrator designated a small conference room for our use. The room was ten feet by ten feet, with a table in the middle and several chairs—just enough room for our team and a couple of computers. Being denied the use of jury questionnaires, as well as prior access to jury lists and information, we knew we would have to rely upon instant research and the skills of our volunteer staff. Fortunately, both Dorothy Sims and my wife Shirley are bona fide computer experts and were more than capable of rising to the challenge.

The process in the courtroom began with the judge announcing himself and having groups of approximately fifty jurors brought in at a time to hear the general instructions of the court. The judge would then read the indictment to them, informing them that this was the case of the State of Florida versus Casey Marie Anthony. This would elicit sighs, strange faces, nods, "I told you so" expressions and the like. Casey, seated at the counsel table between Mr. Baez and me, drew innumerable stares.

We would then begin our questioning. In order to protect the jury candidates, and to encourage greater truthfulness in their responses, we brought them into the courtroom one at a time. Candidates were assigned numbers so as to avoid having to reveal their names, and the media was prohibited from photographing or videotaping their faces.

I had pointed out to Judge Perry in our discussion of jury selection that the biggest and most important obstacle to selection would be the practical hardships faced by these prospective jurors. If selected, they would be bussed to Orlando and sequestered in a hotel, away from their jobs and families, for an estimated two to three months for the trial—all at a paid rate of only $15 a day. Sure enough, during the selection one after another of the candidates expressed resistance to these conditions. I do not know the exact statistics, but I would estimate that seventy to eighty percent of our dismissed jurors were excused on these grounds.

The second area to explore, naturally enough, was prejudgment and exposure to the media surrounding the case. The case had captured the airways, print media and social media of the country for months, and for someone to be completely unaware of it meant that they didn't watch television, didn't read newspapers and might not know whether the United States was at war or not. Not surprisingly, a significant number of jurors admitted that they had already adopted opinions on the case from the media, and had even decided Casey was guilty. The prosecutors, upon such admissions, would frequently try to "rehabilitate" these jurors from the causal challenge immediately issued against them by the defense and try to get them to mitigate their opinions— usually to no avail.

Searching out these prejudices was easier in certain cases than in others. Anyone who admitted that they watched *Nancy Grace*, for instance, was immediately flagged for a causal challenge and questioned in greater depth as to the prejudices engendered by that program. On one occasion, we noticed that Ms. Grace herself was in the courtroom, along with numerous other media celebrities. During a round of questioning that was already going very well, I said to the prospective juror, "Ma'am, I realize that the question I'm about to ask you, and your answer, may prove to be very embarrassing to yourself; but remember, no one here knows your name, nor can they see your face, and I do need to know the answer." The room went utterly silent. I delayed a few seconds before asking, "Ma'am, as hard as it might be to admit, do you watch

Nancy Grace?" At that, the woman smiled and said, "No." There was a burst of spontaneous laughter in the courtroom, and Ms. Grace stormed out, slamming the door.

Another extremely important aspect of the jury selection process in this case was the issue of the jurors' individual feelings about the death penalty. As of this writing there are only, I think, seventeen states that still support the death penalty, and there are huge divisions between rational people over if and when it should ever be imposed. There are those who are categorically against it in all circumstances; conversely, there are those who favor it in all homicide cases. Most people fall somewhere in between.

During our selection, the instant a juror said he or she was in favor of the death penalty, they were wanted by the prosecution. If they said they did not believe in the death penalty and could not impose it, and held this position through questioning, they were disqualified. Throughout this process, the defense team had a dual and almost conflicting set of goals. On the one hand we wanted very much to focus on establishing Casey's innocence and having her acquitted. At the same time, however, we had to explore our options and prepare a safety net for if things went badly. If she was convicted, she would be exposed to the process of a penalty phase; so we needed to try to find jurors who, though willing in general to impose the death penalty, would be unlikely to impose it in this case.

In searching out these ideal candidates, we also uncovered a number of what I call "stealth jurors"—people who secretly want to be on a jury in order to bring a personal agenda to bear. Jurors are required to tell the truth in response to all selection questioning, including the questions whether they know of any reason why they should not sit on the jury, whether they want to be on the jury, and if so, why; but this did not prevent a few from bending the truth a little to hide their personal prejudices. A number of prospective jurors lied about their knowledge of the case, and investment in its outcome. Online research provided other revelations: one juror had a Facebook page on which he had announced that he would do and say whatever was necessary to get on this jury, as he was planning to write a book about it; another was disqualified when it was discovered that he was selling a model electric chair on eBay.

In a particularly remarkable set of circumstances during the first week or so of jury selection, Ms. Burdick, the lead counsel for the prosecution, had thought she recognized the handwriting and perhaps the name of one prospective juror. She thought that this particular lady had been one of the numerous Texas Equusearch volunteers who had searched the area of Suburban Drive where the remains were ultimately found, whom we had uncovered during the deposition process.

When Ms. Burdick told us about her suspicions and we had the woman brought in for private questioning, it turned out that she had indeed been a Texas Equusearch volunteer, but had decided it wasn't important enough to reveal during the questioning process. Moreover, it turned out that she had contaminated the fifty-plus people in her jury pool by talking during breaks with other prospective jurors about her experience with Texas Equusearch and the things she "knew" about the case. She, and her entire jury pool, were summarily excused.

Such admissions were not always damning, however. One of the most revealing prospective jurors acknowledged early on that he had indeed formulated an opinion of the case beforehand. On follow-up, he further admitted that his opinion was that Casey was guilty, but immediately followed this with the rhetorical question, "But of what?" This struck me as the action of a man who was intellectually honest, so while the prosecution thought we were going to excuse this juror—thoughts that were also in my own camp—I insisted upon keeping him. He turned out to be the foreman of the jury that acquitted Casey; given that she was only convicted of misdemeanor charges of lying, his "Of what?" was remarkably apposite.

It took a lot of time and effort to select our jury, but we finally succeeded: twelve men and women as jurors, plus five alternates. Thereafter, the jurors were sequestered in a hotel. They were not allowed to watch television, except for selected programs that limited what they could view. They were not allowed to watch the news. They were not allowed to use a telephone to call their families, except on specific occasions approved by the lawyers and the court. They were not allowed to have computers or smartphones. One wonders if the experience might have been therapeutic for them. When they were brought to the courthouse, there would be picketers with signs outside trying to influence and insult them; yet the jurors were protected from these catcallers too, and never saw them. The rest of us should have been so lucky.

After we were able to complete the jury selection process, it was time to leave Clearwater. We had been gone from Orlando and my office for approximately three weeks. I had heard various reports, and seen a few flashes on the news, of the "media city," sometimes dubbed "Casey Town," that had sprung up like a field of mushrooms across the street from the Orlando courthouse. Despite this early warning, to see it firsthand was overwhelming.

Dozens and dozens of multi-hundred-thousand-dollar motorhome and van conversions ringed the courthouse. Two undeveloped commercial lots— one on the south side of the courthouse and one directly across the street on the west side—had been rented out to various news outlets and were now occupied like some kind of war-torn ghetto. The utility and phone companies had had to put in additional special lines just to accommodate the volume of demand from the media, and actual stages had been built around the courthouse for interviews. Parking places downtown were at an absolute premium. I was later told by a number of different media personalities that even parking their smaller vans on either of the lots around the courthouse had cost them three hundred dollars per day.

I don't know how many hundreds of media people were present there; I saw them everywhere, like ants. And like ants, they had their scouts, who would stand out on the corners across from the building where my office was, and on the corner of the courthouse across the street. As soon as we exited the building in the morning these scouts would relay the information and an army of camera-brandishing soldiers would emerge from behind trees, around the corners of buildings, out of cars, trucks and vans, and wherever else—just to catch us walking across the street, lugging boxes and wheeled carts into the courthouse.

Upon seeing the depth of the media coverage, we became more concerned about security. My office was across the street from the courthouse and ringed on two sides by the media, which required additional security from the building. Not only did they have to post more guards, but we had to have a special code installed for the elevators that went to my floor, so that only colleagues working in my suite and other authorized personnel could get to the twenty-first floor. It would be this way throughout the entire trial, and for most of the following year as well.

In anticipation of the onslaught of observers, the court administration established a form of lottery to grant tickets to the courtroom for citizens who wanted to attend the public trial. The ceremonial courtroom we were using is huge and beautiful, with a balcony in addition to main-level seating; yet only a limited number of citizens could have access to the proceedings—after all, the priority allotment of seats in the gallery behind the bar was given to the news media. Every morning as the trial began, and throughout its entirety, hundreds of people would line up outside, hoping to get tickets. Photographs were constantly being taken, and cheers and jeers bandied about. Some of the news even showed these people getting into pushing and shoving fights in an effort to maintain their positions in the line.

Throughout the whole process—the three years of motions, hearings and interviews, the interminable jury selection process, the threats, the insults, the catcalls and now, finally, the time for trial—Casey Anthony maintained her reserve and composure.

Every morning during the trial she would be awakened at five o'clock, if she was not already up and waiting, in the same isolation cell at Orange County Jail that she had occupied for nearly three years. She would try to eat whatever was made available to her. Then she would be chained, shackled and handcuffed, and brought from the jail to town, and secretly into the courthouse. She was not able to see the mobs outside the courthouse, nor the demonstrations going on; but she had to know they were there. Had she been admitted to pretrial bond like most defendants, there could have been no possibility of a safe trial; I cannot imagine the savagery that would have befallen her under such circumstances, or the terror that even these relatively secure surroundings must have engendered in her. But Casey had a resolve very few people possess, or ever have opportunity to put to proof. Her life utterly in the hands of others, she never stopped believing in herself, or in us. Now that her time of trial had come, she was ready.

13

The Real War Begins

For many of us, particularly old veterans, the Memorial Day holiday is a major time of celebration. It is a time for reflection upon the most important sacrifices that American citizens have made, and continue to make, to ensure that we enjoy a free society according to the principles set out in the Constitution of our country. This freedom is not simply a matter of "living free," but of recognizing the rights of individuals and our protections, not only from foreign threats, but from what is unfortunately becoming even as insidious as these—threats from our own government.

To many American citizens, the concept of "presumption of innocence" is, at best, elusive. I submit that all of us are guilty of seeing news broadcasts and reading newspaper stories about various incidents and leaping quickly to conclusions of guilt. Hopefully a moment's thought will give rise to some healthy skepticism in this regard. Among the various duties I believe are intrinsic to our freedom as American citizens is the duty to question authority, in whatever form we find it, and this includes the authority we grant to our own media to determine the conclusions we draw about everyday events.

The lack of good citizenship in this sense could not be illustrated more alarmingly than in the case against Casey Anthony. No matter where we choose to start in an analysis of her case, we encounter prejudice, hatred and presumption of guilt. The judges were not immune from such feelings, nor were the hundreds of spectators who camped out and fought to see the spectacle of her trial. It was rare to read any form of journalistic report that in any way left open a suggestion of Casey's innocence. The Memorial Day celebration that fell just before her trial began, and its accompanying awareness of the sacrifices of so many men and women over so many years and so many wars, seemed to be lost in the bustle and overwhelming public sentiment the media had engendered around the issue at hand.

Driving to my office, a trek of slightly over fifteen miles, I felt thousands of thoughts competing for first-place priority in my mind. Once there I met the different members of our team and made sure everybody was ready. I wanted all of us to go together across the street and into the courthouse, hopefully without being separated and left to the mercy of the media frenzy. We tried; but numerous media offenders came forward to invade our little group with notepads, cameras and microphones at the ready. This was the gauntlet that would survive, day after day, for the whole six weeks of the trial.

Once in the courthouse, we had to go through the regular security line and metal detectors so that our briefcases and the like could be scanned. Showing the balance of power, the prosecutors didn't have to go through this line. They simply walked through another—courthouse employees dragging behind them whatever boxes or items they wanted—without so much as a look from security.

I have found this imbalance to be interesting for several years. To be a member of the Florida Bar—as I had been at the time of this trial for almost forty years—one not only has to have achieved one's Juris Doctor degree, but also taken and passed the bar exam. Moreover, a thorough and complete background investigation is required before one is admitted. In my day, this investigation started within the first ninety days of law school and lasted up to three years. The State investigators would even go to the lengths of speaking to surviving first-grade teachers and other figures relevant to the applicant's career. Full standard background checks were also carried out.

By contrast, any person whatsoever can apply for a job as a clerk, secretary or assistant of whatever type to the Clerk's Office, to any administrative agency within the courthouse or to the State Attorney's Office. They do not have to go through any security screening or clearance when they arrive at the courthouse; they just show the ID card that was issued to them when they signed their employment agreement, and in they go.

In the initial phases of this trial, just to get to the courtroom was a physical confrontation. The worst offenders were the television personnel, who forced their way into elevators with their microphones and cameras protruding out at us. More than once we were pushed or struck by one of these instruments as they did so; and after one particularly aggressive confrontation—which was fortunately observed by a sergeant with the sheriff's department—we were able to complain to the court. Of course, Judge Perry had no such concerns, as he had a whole series of concealed stairways and private elevators to travel through, but after the complaint, he made sure the sheriff was able to post deputies at the elevators to keep the media and general public at bay.

Only after we were positioned at our table in the courtroom was Casey brought out from her holding cell and allowed to join us. She looked remarkably good under the circumstances—especially given the fact that she had not been allowed to cut her hair for three years. We had requested permission from the judge to send a hairstylist to Casey in jail, so at least her hair could be decent during the trial, but for reasons known best to himself, Judge Perry would not allow it. Still, we had been able to provide her with clothing that had been donated, both by people on her defense team and from elsewhere; and somehow she was able to fix her hair so that she wouldn't look like the disheveled, caged animal that she might otherwise have appeared if her detractors had had their way.

On the counsel tables in this courtroom there are rules of decorum prominently displayed, setting forth the "thou shalt nots" and the "thou musts" for how to act in the courtroom. Among them are rules prohibiting any sign of approval or disapproval of a witness's testimony, or of various other things that occur in a courtroom, as well as any showing of emotion. This became an important part of Casey Anthony's trial.

There were a number of occasions when Prosecutor Ashton, in his bottomless prejudice against Casey, used these rules to object even to the most basic reminders of her humanity. He complained to the court about my putting my "grandfatherly arm" on Casey's shoulder in times of emotional and difficult testimony, and about the many other shows of emotion that one would expect to see on our side in a trial of such magnitude. For his part, of course, no display of emotion was inappropriate, no matter how flagrantly unprofessional. Throughout the trial he attempted to intimidate Mr. Baez with relentless sneering and laughing—which, luckily for him, Judge Perry couldn't see because of the courtroom setup—and called up a whole range of theatrical affectations on command.

The first part of a jury trial, after the assembling of all of the participants, is the announcement of everyone's identities on record. The judge then reads the indictment against the defendant, then gives the jury some preliminary instructions, essentially to advise them of what's going to happen during the trial, and when. It's a fairly simple, fairly straightforward procedure; however, it triggered the first of many objections that the defense would have to make, and motions we would have to issue, during the course of the trial.

Remember that under our system of laws in the United States, a defendant is not required to prove anything, nor to testify if he or she does not choose to do so. A defendant has the absolute right to remain silent during his or her trial, or, if desired, the absolute right to testify in it. This is another way of saying, as we usually do, that the whole burden of proof rests with the prosecution. They are the only ones required to have a case during trial or present evidence in court to a jury.

In starting this trial, Judge Perry advised the jury that once the State had called its witnesses, and the witnesses were examined and cross-examined, and so on, the defense would present their case. I objected to this, on the grounds that, strictly speaking, the defense does not have an obligation to present any case, and while it was clear that we had prepared and were indeed planning, *if necessary*, to present a defense, it was improper for Judge Perry to tell the jury to expect it. After all, the process in a case like this provides that upon the conclusion of the State's case, the defense is entitled to argue for a judgment of acquittal—that is, they are entitled to tell the judge why they believe there is such reasonable doubt or failure of proof that the case should be dismissed altogether, without being sent to the jury for a decision at all.

This initial skirmish having subsided, the record was made. Now it was time for the opening statements. Many people misunderstand this part of the process and think that an opening statement is intended to represent an opening *argument*. Under the rules, in fact, that's exactly what it cannot be. It is supposed to be a statement of what the lawyers expect in good faith that their evidence will reveal, upon proper presentation to the jury. Some analogize it to a roadmap, by which one tells the jury how they're going to get from Point A to Point B, and what they will see and hear along the way.

The State goes first—or more accurately, because the State is the only side *required* to make an opening statement, it goes first. Some defense lawyers, in special circumstances, have elected not to make an opening statement, although I have never tried a case in which I thought that was appropriate. Without a statement from the defense, the State's one-sided presentation to the jury almost certainly paves the way for a prosecutorial victory, if only by being the sole set of expectations placed in front of them.

In the opening statements by the prosecution against Casey Anthony, they told the jury that the evidence would prove that Casey had murdered her child in a premeditated fashion that justified the death penalty they would seek against her. They claimed they could prove that Caylee Anthony had been suffocated with duct tape—a change from the theory they had encouraged the media to propagate up to this point, of poisoning by chloroform—and went on, over vigorous objections by the defense, to paint a picture of Casey's bad character, apparently thinking it sufficient grounds for the death penalty that the twenty-two-year-old girl had been caught going out to nightclubs. They made a great point of dwelling on the length of time Caylee had been missing, as though this too were sufficient proof of Casey's murderous character.

Mr. Baez then rose to make the opening statement for the defense: in essence, that Caylee Anthony had drowned in a pool, and that her remains had been concealed under the direction of Casey's father, George Anthony, whose alleged sexual abuse of his daughter underlay the character of her reactions during the time of Caylee's absence. This was far from the first time this explanation had been explored in court, or presented to the media. I had confronted the prosecution's star medical examiner with the pool-drowning hypothesis a year and a half previously, during her deposition; and the issue of alleged sexual abuse had arisen in the press via jailhouse letters and through psychiatric interviews with Casey. Yet when Mr. Baez had finished with his statement, virtually all of the media present behaved as though it were the first time they had ever heard it. Taking it as a newly concocted scheme, they were quick to conclude—and their talking-head contributors quick to confirm—that the defense was desperate, and Casey's guilt all but confessed.

Thus the trial began; and if there had not been a sufficient quantity of obstruction of justice up to this point, it would soon begin to unload in earnest.

The prosecution called George Anthony as its first witness. Whether this had been planned all along or was improvised on the spot, Mr. Anthony was put on the stand, essentially to testify in rebuttal to the opening statement rather than in any meaningful presentation of evidence.

Ordinarily, under the general Rule of Sequestration, a witness would never be present to hear what had been said before his arrival. This is a very reasonable precaution, taken to ensure that the witness's testimony will not be altered in response to what has gone on before their arrival. However, this being the "Case Against Casey," Mr. Anthony had been allowed to remain in the courtroom with his wife and had heard Mr. Baez's entire opening statement. His testimony, elicited directly by Mr. Ashton, was that he was appalled by Mr. Baez's statement, that he had never heard such allegations before and that they made him sick to his stomach. Upon hearing this, I'm quite sure I broke the rule against showing any reaction to witness testimony, because frankly, I was astonished.

The fact is that Mr. Anthony, Mr. Ashton and all of the prosecution team had *long* been aware of the allegations of sexual abuse—around two and a half years. As I've mentioned, the allegations originally surfaced in jailhouse letters that Casey had exchanged with other inmates. Interestingly, mutual confidentiality being the agreement among these inmates, none of the letters were ever meant to have seen the light of day; yet one of the other women had determined, with the aid of her family, that perhaps they ought to be saved against the event that she might be able, as she said, to "go on Oprah."

Before the letters were to be publicly revealed, the court had graciously allowed the defense two weeks to review their approximately two hundred and fifty pages to determine whether or not there might be any content within them that was subject to proper legal objections and protections from the public, such as attorney-client discussions or other privileged matters. During that time, Mr. Baez and I had asked to speak to George and Cindy Anthony about the content and release of the letters to see their reaction and to elicit a response from them that had not been forthcoming so far. Arrangements were made for them to appear in my office to discuss the case against their daughter with us, with their lawyer ready on call.

In an effort to have some spontaneous and candid conversation, I had asked for George to come into my office alone, while Cindy waited out in the reception room. Once he was there, I had told him "man to man," and as a father and grandfather, that I felt that it would be best to tell him what was going to occur on the following Monday, the date that had been set for the letters' release. I had then looked him in the face and told him the allegations that had been made against him. I had been surprised to see almost no reaction. After a few seconds, I had recognized the unusual "non-response" and looked at my watch to time the delay—an old courtroom tactic. From the time I had looked at the face of my watch, it had been a full twenty-four seconds before any reaction had come from Mr. Anthony; at which point his response had simply been to turn slightly to the side, slap both of his palms on his thighs and let out a sigh. I had then asked Jose to go out to the reception room and have Cindy join us, at which point we had related the allegations to her, whereupon she had cried, protested, and exchanged looks with her husband in what had to have been one of the most uncomfortable situations of my career.

Now, knowing this certainly made Mr. Anthony's opening testimony for the prosecution incredible, but the degree to which this "shocking" information had in fact been known to him in advance went even further than that. Casey had revealed the same allegations in much more detail in psychiatric interviews arranged by her defense, whereupon Mr. Ashton had taken deposition testimonies of each of the doctors involved. At this point he knew very well what Casey had claimed; furthermore, against the express direction of the court—but as I've mentioned, with no corresponding sanction or rebuke—he had promptly met with George and Cindy to tell them everything that had been revealed in the depositions.

So now, despite the clear and inescapable fact that Mr. Anthony had not only heard the allegations against him, but had likely talked with his lawyer about them and had them described from sealed deposition notes, he was being presented by the prosecution as Witness Number One to proclaim his shock, under oath, to the court.

As the State went on, it became evident that their intent was to besmirch Casey's character, rather than present substantial evidence against her. They next called over a dozen of Casey's prior friends and boyfriends to testify about Casey's having gone to parties, worked part-time in a nightclub, and lied about her employment at Universal. Of course, none of them had anything materially relevant to say about Casey; under cross-examination, none of them testified to having seen any evidence of parental abuse or neglect of Caylee. None of them knew anything about Caylee's disappearance, or had any reason to believe that Casey had anything to do with it, other than that she seemed not to have shown sufficient evidence, or what the prosecution accepted as evidence, of grief in their presence. This supposed proof of bad character was to be more or less the substance of the prosecution's entire case.

Having put forth this entirely imaginative and prejudicial appeal at the outset, the State then attempted to support it on a foundation of junk science. Despite conflicting evidence and the direct testimony of several law enforcement officers that they had not smelled any "odor of death" in the car, the State did its level best to salvage that idea by similar imaginative appeals. They trotted out the commonplace and unscientific "once you smell it, you never forget it" claim once more, despite overwhelming evidence against it; then brought in an entomologist to link a single blowfly leg, found in the trunk of the car, to the decomposing body they had conjured up there. Never mind the bag of garbage that had undisputedly been there; what the imagination could supply was far more compelling.

Next came the issue of the discovery site, and the infamous duct tape stuck to Caylee's jaw. Lacking fingerprints, DNA evidence, or any other substantiating evidence, the prosecution again relied on imaginative appeals; yet this time it was to their advantage not only to call up new images in the jury's mind, but to hide facts from them as well. Remember that one of the major issues relating to the discovery of Caylee's remains was how long they had been where they were found. If the remains had been placed there at a time when Casey was in jail, then she could not have done it, and there had to have been participation by another party. This was a fact too glaring to be covered up by the prosecution, so instead, they did everything they could to make it seem as if the remains had been there the whole time, despite all the search efforts and claims to prior discovery, previously discussed. Yet it was in their effort to establish the duct tape as the murder weapon that the prosecution reached what was perhaps its most egregious level of obstructive behavior yet, in their interference with one of the defense's key witnesses.

I should remind the reader here that an overriding, and quite fundamental, aspect of our system of justice is what is known as an adversarial proceeding. This is the concept that both sides in a trial must present their evidence according to common rules, according to which the judge is also required to sort out that evidence and act to ensure a fair presentation to the jury. There is not supposed to be any gamesmanship used to trick the jury, or to hide or distort the truth of what is being shown to them. Jurors, for their part, are not expected to be lawyers or scientists. They are expected to be honest, open-minded, intelligent people able to make decisions about evidence properly presented to them in accordance with the established rules of trial.

It is worth repeating in this connection that prosecutors, along with their authoritative power in front of a jury, bear a special burden in our system to ensure fair play and a proper presentation of the facts. Their job is not to contrive methods of presenting corrupt testimony, or of concealing valid and proper testimony. Moreover, under Florida law, any person who knowingly uses intimidation, or attempts to do so, in order to induce a witness to be absent from official proceedings or to avoid testifying when subpoenaed may be found guilty of tampering with witnesses—a crime punishable, when committed in connection with a capital case, by life in prison.

Being mindful of the State's theory of the duct tape having been used to suffocate Caylee Anthony, we of the defense found it incumbent upon us to disprove the basics of this theory. Accordingly, we presented a great deal of evidence to the contrary, initially in the form of the testimony of Dr. Werner Spitz, who had made it clear that, due to the lack of DNA evidence or fingerprints, the tape could not be proven as Mr. Ashton's "murder weapon."

We had also obtained the cooperation of Dr. William Rodriguez, a forensic anthropologist who had been employed for decades by the U.S. Department of Defense Armed Forces Medical Examiner's Office. His testimony, devastating to the prosecutorial argument, was that it would be impossible to determine the exact original position of duct tape on a decomposed body such as Caylee's. The tape would have lost its stickiness and shifted due to the decomposition process and to external variables, particularly the actions of local wildlife.

Dr. Rodriguez had submitted a report before the trial but had not specifically articulated his position regarding the duct tape. Remember that Judge Perry had directed that, if the lawyers did not take the sworn deposition testimony of an expert, and if a particular subject was not specifically included in that expert's written report, that expert would not be allowed to testify to it. I had objected to that process, being mindful that it would invite the prosecution to purposefully avoid taking depositions in an effort to thwart the defense's presentation of the whole truth. In this situation, that is exactly what Mr. Ashton did.

When we called Dr. Rodriguez to the stand, Mr. Ashton objected, claiming that Mr. Baez had failed to comply with the pretrial ruling regarding expert witnesses. On our plea to the court that this was a death-penalty case, and so required the presentation of all evidence, the judge, perhaps seeing through the gamesmanship being attempted by the prosecution, allowed Dr. Rodriguez to be passed over so that Mr. Ashton could finally take his deposition—as he had had months to do previously.

The court recessed for that purpose, and we spent several hours that Saturday afternoon with Mr. Ashton, questioning Dr. Rodriguez under oath. It was clear that Dr. Rodriguez possessed unassailable credentials and expertise. His deposition testimony was straightforward, professional, candid, articulate—and very damaging to the prosecution. He was unswervingly clear, despite Mr. Ashton's repeated attempts to pressure him, that the duct tape could not have been the prosecution's desired "murder weapon."

The defense felt relieved that we would now be able to get back to the trial. We had the next day, a Sunday, off, during which we prepared for Monday with the great anticipation of putting Dr. Rodriguez on the stand to repeat his testimony to the jury.

But the prosecution's game was not yet over. Despite Mr. Ashton's over thirty years' experience as a prosecutor, he claimed to the court on Monday morning that he needed more time to review his notes in preparation for the cross-examination of Dr. Rodriguez. Incredibly, and over objection, the court granted his plea for additional time.

Now this request for time, it turned out, had a shocking rationale behind it. The Sunday between his deposition and his scheduled court testimony, Dr. Rodriguez had received, by great coincidence, a call from his boss, who told him that he needed to return to Washington and that if he was not there on time because he was testifying in this case, he would be fired. His twenty-plus-year career would be over, and his income—as well as insurance protection for his critically ill wife—would be gone.

After having met privately with Dr. Rodriguez to discuss the horrendous dilemma he was facing, we talked with the judge about it and had a court conference. Remarkably, during this conference, Mr. Ashton revealed that he, too, had had a call with Dr. Rodriguez's boss on Sunday, who had called him on his cell phone. Now this was a remarkable circumstance! How would Dr. Rodriguez's boss have access to Mr. Ashton's cell phone in the first place? And why would he call him on a Sunday to discuss anything, much less Dr. Rodriguez's testimony?

Obviously, we were placed in quite a spot. We discussed the situation again with Dr. Rodriguez and, of course, with Casey, whose humanity was clear despite the importance of the doctor's testimony. "We cannot do that to Dr. Rodriguez," she said; so, backed into a corner, we let Dr. Rodriguez go, and lost an important defense witness to the deceptive efforts of the prosecution.

As it would turn out, the deception was even more egregious. Mr. Ashton later stated that the phone call with Dr. Rodriguez's boss had actually taken place on Saturday, *before* the doctor's deposition was taken—which meant that Ashton had gained the advantage of this information and had kept it from us in order to play out the time of the deposition, claim time to review notes and watch us lose our witness.

Lis Fryer and I discussed the possibility of filing a Motion for Mistrial on the grounds of prosecutorial misconduct and obstruction of justice. Again in consideration of Dr. Rodriguez, we never filed it; but Lis did prepare the motion, which I reproduce here, as follows:

IN THE CIRCUIT COURT FOR THE NINTH JUDICIAL CIRCUIT
IN AND FOR ORANGE COUNTY, FLORIDA

STATE OF FLORIDA,   CASE NO.: 482008-CF-0015606-O
     Plaintiff,   Judge Perry

vs.

CASEY MARIE ANTHONY,
     Defendant.
_____/

MOTION FOR MISTRIAL AND/OR MOTION TO DISMISS BASED ON INTENTIONAL PROSECUTORIAL MISCONDUCT

COMES NOW the Defendant, CASEY MARIE ANTHONY, by and through her

undersigned Counsel and moves this Court to declare a mistrial and in addition or in the

alternative grant a motion to dismiss and, in support, states the following:

"A motion for mistrial should be granted when it is necessary to ensure that a defendant

receives a fair trial." *Morton v. State*, 972 So. 2d 1088 (Fla. 5th 2008) (citing *Power v. State*, 605

So. 2d 856 (Fla. 1992). Further:

> "[T]he granting of a motion for a mistrial made by the defense ordinarily does not
> bar a retrial, even where the error was due to action of the state." *State v. Balezos*,
> 765 So.2d 819, 822 (Fla. 4th DCA 2000); see *Fuente v. State*, 549 So.2d 652,
> 657-58 (Fla.1989). A narrow exception exists, however, when the State's
> misconduct was intended to provoke the defendant into moving for a mistrial. See
> *Gibson v. State*, 475 So.2d 1346, 1347 (Fla. 1st DCA 1985) (stating that for
> double jeopardy to attach after a mistrial due to prosecutorial misconduct, court
> must find that prosecution intended to "goad" defendant to move for mistrial).
> Only under such a scenario of intentional prosecutorial misconduct, will double
> jeopardy attach. See *Fuente*, 549 So.2d at 658 ("Only where the governmental
> conduct in question is intended to 'goad' the defendant into moving for a mistrial
> may a defendant raise the bar of double jeopardy to a second trial after having
> succeeded in aborting the first on his own motion." quoting *Oregon v. Kennedy*,
> 456 U.S. 667, 676, 102 S.Ct. 2083, 72 L.Ed.2d 416 (1982)); see also *Rodriguez v.
> State*, 622 So.2d 1084 (Fla. 4th DCA 1993) (finding that retrial did not violate
> double jeopardy because prosecutorial misconduct, although present, was not
> intentional).

Mr. Ashton has engaged in purposeful behavior which has violated Casey Anthony's right to a fair trial. As a result, declaration of a mistrial is necessary to avoid an injustice.

Further, the intentional prosecutorial misconduct was, at a minimum, an attempt to illicit a mistrial. If this is not the case, then the misconduct was an attempt to deprive the Defendant of her due process rights in a case in which the State is seeking the ultimate sanction. As a result, the Court must dismiss the charges against Ms. Anthony because, under the circumstances, double jeopardy has attached. *Scurry*, 933 So. 2d 565-66.

One thing that perhaps remains as an anchor for those who categorically refuse to accept the trials' ultimate verdict is the matter of the chloroform. This was a lightning rod for media speculation during Casey's trial, and seemed to many to be the key to the prosecution's case. Yet this, like the rest of their supposed evidence, would fall apart under scrutiny.

Right from the beginning there was a confusion in the prosecution's theory as to what role chloroform might have played in Caylee's death. What mattered to them was simply that chloroform—with all its murderous implications—had been involved; how it had been involved was never consistently argued. Sometimes chloroform had been used to poison Caylee, either singly or prior to her suffocation with duct tape; at other times it was relevant as one of the supposed elements of decomposition found in the trunk of the car. Mr. Ashton, for his part, remained confused right through his closing argument, but this didn't stop him from bringing in still more spurious evidence in his attempt to sway the jury. In the end he held to his theory, even despite the following:

a. There was no chloroform, or ingredients to make chloroform, found in the Anthony home.
b. There was no chloroform found on Casey's person, any of her clothes or anything close to her.
c. There was no chloroform found in the child's remains.
d. There was no chloroform found on the child's car seat, on her doll or on the car's steering wheel.
e. Chloroform, at least in Florida, is routinely found in drinking water; it's also found in soda cans, swimming pools—and glues used to put carpets in trunks.

f. The claim that chloroform *was* found in the car is based solely on substance determinations made using a gas chromatograph mass spectrometer. Even then, an FBI agent, refuting the prosecution's lab worker, said that its levels were "very, very low." The other chemists and experts involved said what was found was meaningless. Dr. Arpad Vass claimed that the chloroform levels found in his lab's tests were "unusually high," but he didn't measure precisely how much chloroform there was—and he isn't a chemist.

g. There was one chemist—the State's toxicology witness, Dr. Goldberger—who had told me during deposition that chloroform was a very volatile substance. On the deposition table was a small container with a little lid on it. I asked Dr. Goldberger what would happen, given this volatility, if the container had chloroform in it and I took the lid off. His testimony was that the chemical would dissipate *immediately*—as of course it also would have, had it ever been in the trunk of the Anthonys' car to begin with.

Up against so overwhelming a volume of truth, the State then produced computer experts to claim that someone had used the Anthony home computer to search for the subject matter "chloroform" a total of 84 times. This information, it may well be imagined, rocked the airwaves, and continues to sit foremost in the memory of those who remain convinced of Casey Anthony's guilt.

Of course, upon a little reflection, the idea becomes slightly less plausible. Why would anyone, even with the most egregious intent to do harm, search 84 times for it online, in such a short matter of time, and for such remarkably brief durations as the State claimed? Something seemed shaky about it; it wasn't long before we found out why.

The software used by the State to support their assertion of the 84 searches, a program called CacheBack, was invented and provided by a Canadian programmer, Mr. John Bradley, who was called by the State to give expert testimony. During his testimony, Dorothy sensed that something was wrong. She felt that Mr. Bradley wasn't quite comfortable about his software and wasn't saying everything he had to say about it. Mr. Baez, not wanting to go too far afield in his cross-examinations, let it drop; but Dorothy couldn't.

Her intuition was so clear that later, after the closing arguments, she tried to call Mr. Bradley to talk to him. Mr. Bradley refused to speak to her; although in declining, he seemed to her to be very upset, and gave her the excuse that in Canada, experts are not allowed to talk to the "other side." Dorothy could tell that he wanted to say something further, but that he felt he could not unless he had permission from Linda Drane Burdick to do so.

We walked around in the area where all the lawyers were mulling around, and Dorothy found Linda to talk to her. Dorothy dialed Mr. Bradley's number and tried to get Linda to grant him permission to talk with her, which Linda immediately refused without explanation. Now we knew something was wrong. My prior experiences with Linda, as I mentioned earlier, had never shown her in this light.

Sitting right next to Linda on one of the benches outside the courtroom, Dorothy leaned over and asked her point-blank if the State had any reason to believe that there had not actually been 84 "chloroform" searches. Linda's only answer was, "We're looking into it." Dorothy was relentless, and continued to press her, asking if in fact the State had evidence that there really had *not* been 84 searches for chloroform. Linda mouthed a vague response, without being direct. Again Dorothy demanded to know what the State knew, and Linda answered that she would let her know once she had gotten something confirmed in writing.

Dorothy was livid. After this last confrontation she came running into the courtroom where Jose and I were sitting and told us of their conversation. It was apparent to all of us that if there had been no problems with the testimony, Linda would have been much more direct in her response.

A *New York Times* article published on July 18th, 2011 confirmed our suspicions on this matter. The article asserts that the prosecution's claim that Casey Anthony conducted extensive computer searches on the word "chloroform" was inaccurate. This inaccuracy was confirmed and reported by John Bradley, chief software developer of CacheBack. Mr. Bradley states that after redesigning his software, it was clear that someone performed only one search of the word "chloroform" through Google, not 84 as the prosecution had previously stated. The website that was visited, sci-spot.com, provided information on the use of chloroform in the 1800s. Mr. Bradley said he alerted prosecutor Linda Drane Burdick and Sgt. Kevin Stenger of the Sheriff's Office in late June to tell him of his discovery, but his findings were never presented to a jury and the record was never corrected.

"I gave the police everything they needed to present a new report," Mr. Bradley said. "I did the work myself and copied out the entire database in a spreadsheet to make sure there was no issue of accessibility to the data."

In the article, Mr. Bradley says he became suspicious of the data after his testimony on June 8. He said that while he had been called to testify about his CacheBack software, he had instead been repeatedly asked about the Sheriff's office report that detailed the 84 "chloroform" searches, which he was not familiar with. After giving his testimony, Mr. Bradley learned about the report the police had written in August 2008 detailing this internet history. That report, however, used a different software, NetAnalysis. This report said that there was only one "chloroform" search. After some redesigning and analyzing, Mr. Bradley found that both reports were inaccurate, although the Net-

Analysis came up with the correct result. His more thorough analysis showed that the Web site, sci-spot.com was only visited by someone once.

To assure any skeptics that there is no question as to the truth and validity of the *New York Times* article, following is a post by SiQuest from July the 11th, which describes in great detail, the timeline of Mr. Bradley's testimony.

FOR IMMEDIATE RELEASE
Monday, July 11, 2011

Computer Evidence in the Casey Anthony Trial - A Post Mortem

ADVANCED INTERNET CACHE AND HISTORY ANALYSIS

In the recent case of the State of Florida vs. Casey Anthony, a recovered Firefox 2 history from Unallocated Space became the focal point of the State's case surrounding arguments of "premeditation". During the course of the trial, two different reports were tendered by members of the Orange County Sheriff's Department (OCSD). One was created using NetAnalysis dated August 2008. The other was created using CacheBack Version 2.8 RC2 in December 2009.

What came out at trial was a discrepancy between the two reports with regards to the Visit Count of 84 visits a "chloroform.htm" at "sci-spot.com". The NetAnalysis report was tendered by the Defense under Direct Examination of OCSD's lead forensic examiner. The CacheBack report had already been tendered by the State during Direct Examination of the developer of CacheBack (me) one week earlier.

As a result of this "discrepancy", a lot of confusion and presumptions have arisen. The first presumption is that NetAnalysis was the "correct report" and CacheBack was faulty. While admittedly true that CacheBack had some issues with the Visit Count and was missing some records, BOTH software products failed to fully parse the entire mork database file by some few hundred records.

On July 11, 2011, Digital-Detective.co.uk posted a public blog to discuss the discrepancy issue and provided a tutorial on the Mork file format in contrast to "the other tool". Since the article refers to the Casey Anthony trial and the issue at hand, the author might as well have simply said "CacheBack" and be straight about it. As a result, I feel compelled to set the record straight once and for all. I therefore need to shed some light on exactly what transpired that led to the issues at hand.

The following is a timeline of events that took place since the beginning of the investigation through to and including the final days of the trial:

1. **AUG 2008** - NetAnalysis was used to parse the Firefox 2 history file that OCSD recovered from Unallocated Space. This report listed 8,878 records. The actual mork file contained 9,075 records. This report was disclosed as evidence.

2. **DEC 8, 2009 (16 months later)** - While attending a CacheBack course in Orlando, members of the OCSD stated that NetAnalysis was NOT able to parse the FF2 file. They also cited issues with Daylight Savings conversion with the tool. CacheBack 2.8 at the time could only parse part of the file so I was asked to try and re-tool the function so that it could fully parse the FF2 file.

3. **DEC 10, 2009** - I completed the updates to the best of my abilities at the time for CacheBack 2.8 RC2 and turned over the results to OCSD. I urged OCSD to manually validate select artifacts in the file since they had the Firefox 2 file format and decoding instructions from the CacheBack course Training Manual. I asked that any issues or concerns be brought to my attention immediately for investigation and/or correction. Since Firefox 2 history (mork) file format was already deprecated, I felt at that time that no additional work was warranted on "that specific file format". In hindsight, I should have re-verified the work upon my return to Canada but that was unfortunately not the case.

4. **OCT 2010** - I was deposed as a witness in the case with the State and Defense counsels present. My line of questioning was completely restricted to my actions from December 2009. At NO time was I ever asked to "analyze" or "investigate" the history data or form any opinions. At NO time in the future was I also asked to analyze or investigate the history file. My sole purpose was to provide a "decoding function" for the investigators.

5. **MAR-MAY, 2011** - I contacted the State Attorney's office on numerous occasions to verify what I was required to testify about at trial. I specifically inquired about *whether I needed to examine the data*, create any presentations for court, or if I required a laptop. I was told that I did not need to bring anything and that everything was already looked after. I was expected to only be on the stand for a few minutes - that was it.

6. **JUN 8 & 9, 2011** - I was called to the stand by the State to testify about a CacheBack report that I had never seen before and the contents of which I had no foreknowledge of. This report was created by OCSD on June 3rd, 2011! I was only supposed to get up on the stand and say "I decoded the file" and that was it. Instead, I was tediously asked to read directly from the CacheBack report. Since OCSD officers had testified prior to me, and since the State was not affording me an opportunity to 'explain in simple terms' items like "URL" etc., I essentially was just a narrator and assumed that the jury was already educated by OCSD witnesses.

During my testimony, my attention was directed to a URL at "sci-spot.com" and I was asked to read aloud the Visit Count for that entry. As I stated in the courtroom, I said "According to the report...84 times". Personally speaking, a single "chloroform.htm" with a visit count of 84 seemed odd. But, since I did not have any other details about the investigation, and since I did not investigate the evidence, that's all I could say.

7. **JUN 16, 2011** - The supervising OCSD computer forensic investigator (Sergeant) took the stand under direct examination by the Defense. He was shown two reports: the NetAnalysis report from August 2008 (which parsed only 8,878 records) and the CacheBack report, which parsed 8,571 records. OCSD was asked to point out the glaring differences between the Visit Count of 1 for the NA report and 84 for the CB report. In addition, "myspace.com" was missing from the CB report, as were other URLs. Rather than acknowledge this *already known* issue and address it there and then, the officer chose not to.

From a developer's perspective, this was an obvious "parsing error". By looking for a valid Visit Count attribute, CacheBack skipped over records until it found a valid Visit Count marker. As I later determined (see below), FF2 infers the first visit count and thereby "omits" the Visit Count attribute altogether. So while terribly damaging, the actual correction to the problem was relatively easy, and obvious to me once I became aware of it.

8. **JUN 16, 2010 (after his testimony)** - I called the OCSD Sergeant about his testimony and inquired about the discrepancy. That's when he said that he KNEW about this discrepancy LONG AGO. When asked "What did you do about it?", he replied "that he visually inspected the URL within the Firefox 2 history file which was in question and observed the number 84 nearby ("a couple of lines below") and assumed that it was correct". Despite the obvious and critical flaw in this thinking, he still knew that the NetAnalysis report was still in evidence with a visit count of 1.

According to the OCSD officer, this discrepancy was known LONG before trial. NO attempts were made to contact me, the developer of NetAnalysis or to validate it manually using any other combination third party tools. Validation of "select URLs" (e.g., chloroform) would have taken only 10 minutes. So at this point, there are 2 inconsistent reports before the court and nothing was done about it. Even the prosecutor didn't know.

9. **JUN 16-19, 2011** - I advised the State Attorney of the problem(s) and liased with her and the OCSD officer. During the next 36 hours, I completely retooled the code in CacheBack and successfully matched the proper 9,075 records. An independent tool called "dork.exe" developed by the Mozilla developers corroborated my results. I also used EnCase Version 6 keyword search on the new record marker (a square open bracket) and verified the same results. CacheBack 3.7.11 was immediately released and I prepared an assortment of published results (for OCSD and the State prosecutor) in various file formats to make it easy to disclose and review.

This information was provided to the prosecution and to the OCSD in advance of the State's rebuttal, and the OCSD officer's second appearance (for the State). I even offered to fly down there overnight at my own expense to set the record straight and explain the discrepancy. Since the fate of woman's life could lay in this critical piece of information, I did everything in my power to remedy the situation, or at least mitigate the issue - once I became aware of it.

COMMENTS

1. Had OCSD informed me that NetAnalysis had indeed been able to parse the Firefox 2 history file

in August 2008 (16 months earlier), I would have definitely asked for a copy of the results as a benchmark to my own work in December 2009. This information was selectively omitted in my discussions with OCSD.

2. The OCSD had an opportunity and a responsibility to validate the results, in particular, the URLs that were deemed to be the most critical to the State's case. Had I been asked to revisit the results or aid in the examination of the results, the issues would have been discovered and corrected immediately.

3. In hindsight, I could have (should have) done more upon my return in December 2009 to further review the Firefox 2 parsing routine. Unfortunately, this is a valuable lesson learned. Despite Mork file format being depricated, we should have invested more time to review again the changes made in CacheBack 2.8 RC2.

4. While NetAnalysis and CacheBack were eventually updated to better parse the Firefox 2 file, neither product's reports tendered in the Casey Anthony trial were entirely correct. It is disappointing that NetAnalysis in this case was somehow held out to be otherwise.

5. I was not going to post anything herein because I believed that members of the forensic industry would qualify any suspicions by asking involved stakeholders about the matter - directly. Unfortunately and regretably, either for personal gain or for no other reason than to attempt discredit the CacheBack name, certain limited comments have found their way into public venues through posts and blogs that are completely subjective and misleading.

6. Like anyone other software development company, our software is developed by humans and we have endeavored to correct any and all issues immediately once they are discovered or reported. While we do our best to test, test, re-test and test some more, sometimes that isn't always enough.

7. **My personal thanks to my good friend and colleague Shafik Punja of the Calgary Police Service for pushing me to come forward to define the issues and offer the true perspective on the issues.**

CacheBack is a great tool for Internet investigations! I stand behind the product and I stand behind our customers. When a customer reports an issue, we're on it *right away* and we fix it *right away*, if required. The Casey Anthony Trial was a good experience for no other reason than to experience the American justice system and to be humbled in acknowledging **that "one more test" is never a waste of time.**

TO THE MEMBERS OF OCSD:
I am truly sorry that I was unable to refrain from discussing this issue in a less than positive light. Collectively, we could have done things differently and I know we have all learned from this experience.

Respectfully,

John Bradley
CEO & Chief Software Architect

For more information, visit our website at www.cacheback.ca.

SiQuest Corporation
CacheBack Support Team
Email: support@cacheback.ca
Email: info@cacheback.ca

"Every Bit Counts"

To show what happens when prosecutorial pressure is applied, following this statement was a July 20th amendment, by which counsel for the company and Mr. Bradley announced that the release you've just read had been removed—for fear of litigation.

This series of revelations, in my opinion, proves conclusively that the prosecution in this case was corrupt. Every lawyer who practices criminal law is aware of the decision by the United States Supreme Court in the case of *Brady v. Maryland* in 1963, which states that the government is required to reveal to the defense *any and all* evidence that may tend to be exculpatory—that is, that may cast any doubt on the prosecution's case and help prove the innocence of an accused person. This principle, established as United States law, is part of the sworn duty of every prosecutor and police officer in our country. Yet our request to the judge for a special jury instruction to disregard this testimony as erroneous, was declined, and the jury was never made aware that the evidence was completely spurious. Furthermore, to this date there has been no official apology or reprimand for the prosecution's withholding of evidence in Casey Anthony's trial, nor has any local or national media organization that I'm aware of properly explored the situation and exposed it for what it really is.

Had we been afforded the information with which Mr. Bradley came forth after the trial, I submit that we may very well have been entitled to a dismissal of all charges against Casey on the grounds of intentional denial of due process by the prosecution. Of course, whether or not Judge Perry, with his history of ruling in favor of the prosecution, would have undertaken such a motion, we will never know.

There were other witnesses the State did not choose to call to the stand during the trial, whose testimonies would have hurt their case. One of these was the very man who had discovered Caylee Anthony's body—the meter reader, Roy Kronk, whose story would have cast doubt on the date of the body's disposal. Another was the hydrologist they had brought in to corroborate their theory that the area had been underwater when it was searched previously without result—who had found that, in fact, it had not been.

After the State concluded the presentation of its "case in chief," we again had the opportunity to present our own side of the story. There were so many holes in the State's case already that we could not resist putting on a series of witnesses—formerly State witnesses.

For the next two weeks, we presented expert testimony on the foregoing forensic issues, as well as "lay" testimony.

The jury heard from our expert entomologist, who testified that if there had indeed been a body in the trunk of the Anthonys' car, there would have been hundreds or thousands of blowflies trapped in the trunk with it—not merely the leg of one.

Under our examination, the prosecution's medical examiner confessed that she did not know Caylee's cause of death, time of death or place of death, or indeed anything else about her death's occurrence—showing even her initial conclusion, that the death had been a homicide, to be groundless. We brought Dr. Werner Spitz on to further explain that the same medical examiner had failed to do a proper autopsy. Assuming from the beginning, in line with press coverage, that Caylee's death had been a homicide, she had not even opened the child's skull when the body was found.

FBI toxicologists confirmed that no toxic substances were found in any of Caylee Anthony's hair, or dirt similar to that of the discovery site on Casey's shoes or clothes.

The State's own witnesses acknowledged that there had been no blood or incriminating stains found in the Anthonys' car, or on any of Casey's clothes.

A witness testifying that she had had an ongoing affair with George Anthony took the stand and established that George had told her that "Caylee's death was an accident that snowballed out of control."

The truth parade went on and on.

After the presentation of our case, and faced with the glaring likelihood that Caylee had not died as they insisted she had, the State recalled their anthropology expert for one final tug at the jury's imagination. Showing a picture of Casey Anthony smiling and holding her beautiful baby, who was also smiling, they then superimposed a photograph of the child's skull over it, with duct tape Photoshopped across its mouth. Despite the obvious prejudice engendered by this piece of false evidence, and the lack of any scientific grounds for it, all of our objections failed, and Judge Perry allowed it to be shown to the jury.

Fortunately we had a jury smart enough to see through this ruse and the numerous other inappropriate presentations of the prosecution. Yet not all defendants are so fortunate. All too often, convictions of the most serious character hinge upon such thinly-veiled appeals to imagination and prejudice; and amid their wholesale acceptance, the human frailties endemic to our justice system continue to gain footing in legal practice.

It cannot be too often repeated that under our constitutional scheme, a trial is *not* supposed to be a contest for the declaration of a winner. It is fundamental law in the United States, and compelling ethics for the conduct of trials here, that it is not the prosecutor's job to win. It is the prosecutor's job to present *all* of the evidence in a case, not just to select that which helps them win it. The very fact that this has to be said, even to those in the legal profession, illustrates the deterioration of our system of justice.

14

Closing Arguments

For many lawyers and court observers, the closing arguments are among the most important parts of a trial. It is the last time to convince the jurors to interpret the evidence the way you have, and in some cases, to atone for any mistakes that may have been made during the trial. Lawyers on both sides are not necessarily allowed to explain why they did something at the time they were doing it, so the closing arguments provide a chance to bring it all together, and hopefully make some sense.

There are a number of restrictions and rules concerning what one may or may not do during a closing argument. Lawyers are allowed, for instance, to comment on what we anticipate the judge will tell the jury that the law is. But we are also supposed to draw the line between that, and telling them ourselves what *we* think the law is. We're also prohibited from expressing our personal beliefs about evidence to the jury, and particularly from commenting on the credibility of particular witnesses and the guilt or innocence of the accused. If a prosecutor falls into that error, it's virtually guaranteed to result either in a mistrial or in a reversal on appeal. If a defense lawyer does it, he is admonished by the court—and on the few occasions that I've seen it, the chastisement takes place in the presence of the jury.

Lawyers disagree as to what is best to present in jury arguments. There are those who espouse going into great detail, and indeed, some cases do call for a full rehearsal of the facts. However, in my opinion, that doesn't work in the majority of trials. Jurors sit and listen for hours at a time, days and weeks on end; the last thing they want is for somebody to go through a repetition of what they have already endured.

It is my belief that, during this stage of a trial, juries want to hear explanations. Accordingly, a lawyer needs to use this occasion to attempt to anticipate what questions a juror may have, and answer them. Traditionally it has been experience alone that could assist in that process; though we now have a procedure in Florida that allows jurors, under certain restrictions, to write down questions that can be addressed during the trial and closing arguments. I have utilized this process in the past, and while such jury questions can be unnerving, they are certainly revelatory.

As with opening statements, the prosecution goes first in the closing argument process. That is, they get to stand before the jury at the conclusion of the presentation of evidence, argue what they think they have proven and try to convince the jury to agree with their theory. In our case it took the form of an urging—if not an outright plea—by the prosecutors to kill Casey Anthony. That concept should send chills up the spine of any conscientious reader. One would hope that such a profound responsibility as that of a prosecutor would be taken on with the utmost seriousness, and without so overt a show of bloodthirstiness.

Mr. Ashton began by arguing the theory for which no substantial evidence had been presented during the trial at all. He argued to the jury that Casey Anthony had murdered her child—whom, on all other counts, we had every reason to suspect she loved and cared for—simply because she wanted the freedom to party. He went on to support this preposterous theory with the inference they had been feeding the eager news media for nearly three years: because Casey didn't grieve in the manner that they deemed appropriate, she was conclusively a murderess.

Little did Mr. Ashton know that during the course of this very trial there had been two deaths in the families of members of the defense team—through which occurrences those members had carried on with their work every day. Neither of them had come to court with eyes bloodshot from exhaustion, or cheeks stained with tears, though they had loved their grandmother and uncle as much as anybody else. Yet the prosecutor probably wouldn't have cared if he had known. He had his theory and was not going to be deterred by the facts.

As alluded to earlier, Mr. Ashton made some serious faux pas in his argument. Not only was he overzealous in his mythologizing, he couldn't seem to get his theory of the murder straight. Was little Caylee poisoned to death with the chloroform they couldn't find? Or was she suffocated with that other unsubstantiated murder weapon, the duct tape? Confronted with the lack of evidence to support either of these theories conclusively, Mr. Ashton presented both theories to the jury, saying that *in all likelihood* Caylee had been murdered by suffocation. He went on to state, very emotionally, that one could only hope that Caylee had been knocked out by chloroform before she was suffocated with the tape.

Now, the burden of proof in a first-degree murder case, which of course rests with the prosecution, is that the crime must be proven *beyond and to the exclusion of all reasonable doubt.* It is by no means a case for "in all likelihood," or "we can only hope." Interestingly enough, in light of this contradiction and the extremely shaky nature of the evidence upon which his almost entirely prejudicial case was based, Mr. Ashton next had the audacity to deliver an impassioned argument against speculation!

Once Mr. Ashton had finished, Mr. Baez got up to argue the first part of the closing argument for the defense. He chose to go through a lot of facts, but was selective in doing so, revisiting the evidence relevant to those areas in particular in which the jury could find the most reasonable doubt.

During this process, Mr. Ashton could not control himself, and smirked and grimaced and laughed through Mr. Baez's argument. Despite the prosecutor's hundreds of sustained objections, Mr. Baez wasn't afraid of him and called him out on his behavior, pointing to him in front of the jury and referring to him as "this laughing guy here." From his reaction, it was a wonder Mr. Ashton didn't have a coronary occlusion. He physically jumped from his seat and yelled his objection. The judge, predictably, was incensed—but didn't know what had actually happened, as Ashton was where he couldn't see him.

We had yet another bench conference, in which I told the judge what had happened, and Ashton tried to deny it. The judge suggested that we review the courtroom videotape, and despite the fact that neither Mr. Ashton nor Mr. Baez wanted to do so, I insisted on it. We had put up with far too much obstruction up to this point to let the prosecutor off so easily. The judge and I went alone into the media room to review the videotape, where, sure enough, we saw Mr. Ashton—the State prosecutor in a capital case—smirking and degrading the presentation of the defense, and distracting the jury from it, with a big grin on his face.

Judge Perry was justifiably angry—this time at the right person—and I told him my opinion that, in light of the case's history and the repeated efforts by Mr. Ashton to hold Mr. Baez in contempt, fine him and otherwise harass him, it was time for the worm to turn. Fortunately for Mr. Ashton, however,

Mr. Baez let him off the hook, telling the court that he didn't want to belabor the issue and delay getting the trial over with.

After Mr. Baez's portion of the presentation was through, it was my turn. My goal was now to bring the jury to a clear and comprehensive understanding of what is meant by reasonable doubt, and in that fashion point out the problems with the State's case that Mr. Baez had set up in his argument.

By coincidence, the day of these arguments was July the 4th. What a laborious process it had been! We had gone through the presentation of evidence and prosecutorial argument on Memorial Day and were now making our final arguments to the jury on the 4th of July. Yet this was a day, as I reminded the jury, to celebrate our freedom from the oppressions of government, and to honor and respect the constitutional processes and rights that we are so fortunate to have.

I then presented an argument on the subject of reasonable doubt, reminding the jury of the burden of proof that lay upon the prosecution, and following it up with a list of areas in this particular prosecutorial argument for which there was no evidence. It had been a lengthy list, and I reduced it to a reasonably shorthand version; but it was enough to remind the jury of everything we had debated over the last couple of months.

That list simply ran:

- No fingerprints on the tape or bags
- No fingerprints on the gas cans
- No roll of tape found at the Anthony home to match the tape found with Caylee's body
- No toxicology
- No DNA of the defendant

- No evidence of decomposition at the recovery scene
- No bugs from the trunk—only trash
- No chloroform, or ingredients to make it, in the Anthony home
- No heart-shaped sticker in the Anthony home similar to the one found in the vacant lot
- No root bands on the sixteen hairs found in the trunk; the one alleged root band being from a hair not exclusively linked to the defendant
- No connection of the defendant to the recovery scene, despite FBI examination of all of her clothes and shoes
- No incriminating statements, admissions or confessions by the defendant
- No witnesses to the alleged crime
- No motive
- No forensic evidence—i.e., no DNA or blood— from the trunk stain, or anywhere in the car
- No transfer evidence from the car seat, steering wheel cover or anywhere else
- No chemical uniqueness to chloroform as pertaining to decomposing bodies
- No history of child abuse
- No history of child neglect

As I ran down this list, there was no smirking, smiling, laughing, head shaking or other gesturing from the prosecution table. The conscientious jury was giving me their full attention.

I pointed out that the prosecution's imaginative fantasies were not evidence, and that proof "in all likelihood" was not proof beyond a reasonable doubt. I demonstrated the gradations of different classifications of argument strength using a visual aid board (for copies of which, interestingly, I have since had literally hundreds of requests from professors, lawyers, law schools, journalists and generally interested people from all over the country). I spoke to the grave responsibility of the jury in making this momentous decision, and to their power to resist the overwhelming obstruction of justice that had marked the case from its beginning. We had dealt with the media's ignorance, the prosecution's poisonous fantasies, and the court's repeated overruling of our objections and best efforts. Now the case had come to the jury for decision; now it was their turn to decide on what side of justice they stood.

A good friend, author and judge from Miami, Mr. Milton Hirsch, argued in a trial that "today is Judgment Day for the United States Constitution." Tomorrow will be judgment day for the United States Constitution, too. Every day on which an American stands trial for his liberty before a jury; every day on which an American is arrested, or his home or property is searched; every day on which an American voice is raised in speech or song; every day on which an American vote is cast or counted; every day on which an American newspaper is printed or read; every day on which an American lawyer is asked to defend an unpopular man, or an unpopular cause, is Judgment Day for the United States Constitution. We are faced with a storm of injustice, a chaos of oppression, almost continually; yet the judgment is ours. Every one of us, however solitary, is called upon daily for our decision—to cower before the storm, or to light candles in the interest of keeping what is best in us alive.

"Let us light candles," I said—and brought the argument around to its close.

15

The Verdict

After the closing arguments were completed, the judge, as in all cases, instructed the jury on the rules of law pertaining to their deliberations. This is essentially a summary of the elements the State must have proven in order to justify the jury's returning a guilty verdict. (I have always found it interesting that the concept is always worded in this way—"before you can return a guilty verdict"—implying that returning such a verdict is at bottom what juries are there to do.)

One might imagine the contentiousness of the case to have ended with its closing arguments, but in this case, as in others, that was far from the truth. Various further skirmishes and objections took place during what is known as the "charge conference," when the lawyers for both sides meet with the judge to make suggestions of what instructions and guidance are to be given to the jury, and how. Most of these instructions have been standardized now by various court decisions and the rules promulgated by the Florida Supreme Court. However, there is always room for specific suggestions and requests. In our case, for instance, following the discovery of the fraud perpetrated by the State with respect to its fictitious 84 chloroform searches, I requested that the judge specifically instruct the jury to disregard that testimony, and that the State concede that it had been a mistake. Naturally, this suggestion was opposed by the prosecution, but it was harder for me to understand why the judge rejected it. At any rate, the instructions were eventually settled on and delivered, and it was time for the jury to begin its deliberations.

Waiting for the outcome of a presidential election, or for the end of the Kentucky Derby, is anxiety-producing. Waiting for your baby to be born, or for a loved one to emerge from surgery, is agonizing. Waiting for a jury verdict has no parallel in the human experience. I have endured this process well in excess of three hundred times as a lawyer, on one occasion for more than twelve days; and I can tell you, it never becomes easy. It was all we could do that day to get ourselves out through the media barricade and try to keep calm as we awaited the verdict.

The jury returned its decision the next day, after a total deliberation time of about eleven hours. This was a relatively quick verdict on their part, which virtually all of the media personalities and their questionable law analysts interpreted as a "bad sign" for Casey.

Experience had me more uncertain. I knew this was a conscientious jury comprised of dedicated, sensible people. They had paid close attention throughout the trial, and none of them had gone to sleep—a rarer circumstance than one might expect. That such a group could determine the guilt of someone on such shaky evidence, and approve a death sentence for them in such a hurry, seemed unlikely to me. We would probably lose the four misdemeanor counts for lying, but I was more than prepared for that.

Everybody gathered in the courtroom to hear the verdict. Some of the more vituperative press people present were caught on a national news broadcast glaring at Casey and sneering at us in their self-righteousness. Outside, apparently, it was like the 1952 movie *The Day the Earth Stood Still*; I'm told there were a number of traffic accidents due to the announcement.

The jury was escorted in, and immediately the room went silent. I looked at each juror and most of them looked right at me, or at Casey beside me. When I saw this, I started to feel some relief. There is no science to it, but forty-plus years of experience and the hundreds and hundreds of trials that I have been through, as well as the concurring opinion of hundreds of my colleagues with similar experiences both locally and nationwide, have taught me the same thing: if the jury looks at you, you've probably won. When they look away, or refuse to look at the defendant, it's typically a bad sign.

Judge Perry asked everyone to be seated, and then asked—not knowing who the jury foreperson was at this point—whether the jury had reached a verdict or not. The foreman I mentioned earlier stood up and announced that they had. At this I felt another burst of relief, as I knew this fellow was unlikely to do anything haphazardly. I had no way of knowing what the results were going to be, but at least I felt sure it would be the result of a serious and conscientious effort.

In the rather ceremonial procession that follows, the verdict is handed to the deputy, who hands it to the clerk, who hands it to the judge, who reads it first to himself before handing it to his clerk to be read out loud. In this case, again caught by the cameras and broadcast live, you could see the expression of Judge Perry change. He was obviously surprised, and I believe disappointed, by what he was reading. He then handed the verdict to the clerk, who was so shocked that she stuttered and had to begin again in order to clearly pronounce the words "not guilty."

We had saved Casey's life.

Naturally, the clamor from the press was immediate, and deafening. They had all been wrong, at least as far as their predictions went; yet were they embarrassed, or in any way chastised for the vehemence of their prejudgments? Of course not; on the contrary, they started trying to find reasons why everything had gone so terribly wrong. The jury had to be stupid or wrong, they asseverated, or somebody must have bribed them. There was no way the fault could have been in their universal condemnation of Casey, or in the assumptions of their false experts. Even after the verdict had been delivered, the long-settled opinion could not be questioned; which brings us back to our original point, the point of origin for all obstruction of justice, however complex: all human beings are fallible, and most of us hate to admit it.

Immediately following the court's formal adjudication that Casey was not guilty of the serious felony charges against her, and was guilty of the four misdemeanor charges, court was adjourned—but Casey was not yet free. After enduring such an ordeal as she had for so long, many judges would have declared her free right then and there. After all, she had already served three years in jail, much of it in isolation, for which she was entitled to credit. But Judge Perry first kept her until the jailers and clerks could agree upon the number of days that she was entitled to have credited back to her, then maxed her out, giving her the maximum sentence of one year on each of the four counts for which she was pronounced guilty. It is worth pointing out that this has never been done before on such charges—not in Florida, at any rate, and probably not anywhere else. But this was still the "Case Against Casey."

Once Casey had been again chained, handcuffed, shackled on her feet, and taken out the back door and back to jail to await further sentencing, the defense team then convened in the room where the media had gathered. Numerous questions were asked, and I took the opportunity that I had long awaited to reprimand the predators among them for their rapacity and prejudice. Among other things, I recall telling them, "I hope you've learned a lesson"—which was apparently broadcast very widely.

It has not, however, proven very effective, even as the years have elapsed. Nor, I am convinced, are our lessons going to be learned, as long as the news media is allowed to believe that the First Amendment is the only amendment of our Constitution. The other protections of due process are an easy sacrifice to them, and when they are in error, they are never held answerable for it. The worst antagonists of the prejudicial pretrial publicity that surrounded and affected Casey Anthony's trial have not yet admitted, in any capacity whatsoever, that they were wrong; nor have they blamed the prosecution for overcharging the case, or grounding it in flimsy evidence; nor have they even entertained the notion that Casey might in fact be innocent. They have one and all blamed the jury for what they refuse to deem anything but a faulty decision, and in their frenzy to make proof of their right to free speech, still show themselves incapable of exercising the most fundamental and crucial of human freedoms: the freedom to change one's mind.

16

The Fallout

As I write this in the year 2014, nearly three years after the verdict that acquitted Casey Anthony, the case is still controversial. Its emotional shockwaves still reverberate with many people, a fact that, despite my experience in such things, never fails to surprise me. It seems to me to indicate a basic difficulty in accepting facts, or in dealing effectively with the real world; but then again, that the case should be difficult to let go of, even down the line, was established well in advance of the trial by the emotionally incendiary way in which it was billed from the beginning.

Though unfortunate, it was hardly surprising that this fallout should have affected the members of the defense while the trial was going on. Mr. Baez bore the brunt of it. Slandered by the press and under a relentless barrage of sustained objections by the prosecution, he would at times internalize all the negativity even to the point of thinking he was doing Casey more harm than good, and on two separate occasions even considered quitting the team.

Though my experience never allowed me to feel the same degree of despair—and indeed enabled me to call Mr. Baez back from that particular brink—I experienced similar pressures myself, very soon after I began to be publicized in connection with the case. All through the trial I was the target of threats, insults and even direct assaults, as were the other members of the team. Such behavior, sometimes engaged in by members of the legal community itself, affected people even peripherally or temporarily involved with our side.

One such scandal targeted an early member of our team, Professor Andrea Lyon of DePaul University, whom Mr. Baez had brought on to focus on potential death penalty issues. Ms. Lyon, deservedly well regarded by her peers, was a speaker at the aforementioned death-penalty seminar in Orlando jointly sponsored by the Florida Association of Criminal Defense Lawyers and the Florida Public Defenders Association, where she gave a presentation on strategies and prior experiences related to the penalty phase of capital cases.

One of the rules of these presentations is that only defense lawyers are allowed to attend, and they must sign an agreement to maintain the confidentiality of everything that is said there. However, presentations are recorded so that members of the FACDL who are unable to attend the seminar can have access to this extremely valuable information; one lawyer requested the tape of Ms. Lyon's presentation for (as he claimed) personal use. Soon afterward, this recording wound up in the hands of a local television reporter, who immediately spread it around the news in a full-tilt effort to humiliate Ms. Lyon and expose our team's potential defense strategies and concepts for jury selection to the prosecution. The lawyer who had maliciously leaked the tape was allowed to resign from the FACDL, but it seemed a light consequence for so bald-faced an attempt to undermine due process in a capital case.

After the verdict, it took a SWAT team to get the defense team safely out of the courthouse through the outraged mob outside. Would that they had been able to safeguard us so effectively against the hostility that continued to follow us thereafter!

The media's distortion of events has continued, to remarkable depths. On the afternoon of the verdict, when the defense team got together to toast the Constitution—a victory tradition among many defense lawyers—the media outside stooped so low as to broadcast that the defense was celebrating over the death of Caylee Anthony. When I suffered a stroke at a speaking engagement a few months later and had to be hospitalized, the media present followed me to the hospital, attempted to lie their way into the intensive care unit and—when they failed to gain admission—reported that I had died. Speculation and outright falsehood still circulate around the trial and its verdict, and likely will for some time.

Notoriety has brought with it some strange side effects. I, for one, have had a fictitious Facebook page created under my name and at least one false website—which, I'm told, received in excess of 450,000 hits in its first week.

The number of private threats the members of the defense team received, and still receive to this day, is astonishing. At one point the intensity and volume of these threats were such as to warrant formal complaints and referrals to law enforcement, and the Seminole County Sheriff's Department had to assign a team of investigators to look into them. Upon one particularly venomous call to my wife at home, law enforcement responded quickly; and with our consent and appreciation, the sheriff's department has monitored the phone calls to my house ever since. The U.S. Secret Service has also had occasion to investigate the threats we've received, as have the FBI and the U.S. Postal Inspection Service.

This is not to suggest that all of the mail we've received has been bad. In fact, I've kept all the notes, cards and letters we've gotten in "good" and "bad" boxes; and the good messages outnumber the bad approximately eight to one.

These have included unsolicited contributions, large and small, to help defray the trial's expenses, and even anonymous gifts for Casey herself. The latter are particularly appreciated; for unlike the rest of us, Casey's trial is far from over.

The threats against Casey Anthony herself have been so vile and numerous that the young woman still has severe concerns for her life. Since serving her time for her four misdemeanor convictions she has had to remain in hiding, with only a very few knowing her whereabouts. False and malicious—and often completely incompetent—lawsuits have been brought against her, and she has been forced to file a bankruptcy petition to try to have a new start.

After she was freed from the Orange County Jail to begin her present chainless imprisonment, the media's search for her began. I have yet to understand why finding her should be so important to these people—whether they feel that they will get an exclusive interview with her, or intend her harm of some sort, is far from obvious to me—but a great deal of energy and money has apparently already been spent in the pursuit. Groundless rumors that Casey was hiding out in my home have brought helicopters to hover over my house and reporters to invade my neighborhood, some of whom even attempted to solicit my neighbors to spy for them. Even young children in my neighborhood have approached my house to ask if Casey was inside; and the sheriff of Volusia County, where my wife and I own a condominium, called once to tell me he had heard Casey was hiding out there and wondered if I needed extra deputies to patrol the area.

I hope and trust that someday true justice will be served, and Casey Anthony will be able to live a normal life again. Until that time, those who remain on her team are doing all that can be done—and living with the fallout as best we can.

17

Judges and Injustice

In Greek mythology there is a particularly applicable story about a young boy named Icarus, whose father, the great craftsman Daedalus, had been imprisoned in Crete. Daedalus wanted to escape but knew, given the enemy's powerful navy, that he could not do so by ship, so he fashioned wings for himself and his son using bird feathers and wax. Young Icarus was warned that he could not fly too low and close to the sea, as the waves would ruin his wings, nor so high that the heat of the sun would melt the wax and he would plunge to his death. Yet Icarus could not avoid the temptation and flew higher and higher until his father's predictions came true.

Like Icarus, throughout the tale of the "Case Against Casey" we have seen lawyers and judges attempting to fly too high. Today the bright lights of the media are the sun that blinds them to their duty; drawn irresistably to its glare, one by one they have had their wings melted from them. It remains to mention, by way of follow up, two further brushes with this all-powerful sun, made by the two most important authorities attached to the case: its judges.

We have already discussed the media-related removal of the trial's initial judge, Stan Strickland. One might expect that out of professionalism, this would be the end of him with respect to the trial's proceedings; but the day after the verdict, Judge Strickland saw fit to appear on *Nancy Grace*, telling the world, in essence, that the jury "didn't know what he knew" and had rendered a faulty decision.

Now, recall that judges, in addition to being members of the Bar Association and subject to its rules and regulations, are also required to comply with what are known as the Judicial Canons of Conduct. Canon 3 specifically provides several rules particularly applicable to this situation, one requiring the judge to perform his or her judicial duties without bias or prejudice; and another stating simply that the judge shall not be swayed by parties of interest, public clamor or fear of criticism. Having been barred from the trial for his violation of the first of these commandments, Judge Strickland had now gone on to compound that wrongdoing with a violation of the second. Accordingly, complaints were filed against him; shortly afterward, he elected to resign his circuit judgeship.

This, like Judge Strickland's former transgression, was a great disappointment; but it was nothing compared to the disgraceful light Judge Perry, the succeeding judge, would choose to shed on himself at the trial's completion.

On Thursday, May the 2nd, 2013, I received a call from a producer who works with *The Today Show,* whom I had gotten to know fairly well throughout the whole ordeal. He gave me some news that, though pleasing to him, had also surprised him greatly: Judge Belvin Perry was going to appear on *The Today Show* to talk about the Casey Anthony case. I could hardly believe it; judges don't do that. But he assured me that this was the plan.

Indeed, on the following Monday, precisely as predicted, Judge Perry appeared on *The Today Show*, beginning his interview with Savannah Guthrie at 7:32 in the morning. Below is the transcript, verbatim, of that interview.

Ms. Guthrie: Judge Perry, good morning. It's good to see you.

Judge Perry: Good morning, Savannah.

Ms. Guthrie: Well, when you were in the middle of it, did you realize what a sensation all of this was?

Judge Perry: I had no earthly idea that it would command the attention that it did worldwide. It was truly a fantastic experience.

Ms. Guthrie: Well, you had a vantage point very few have, in particular on the defendant, Casey Anthony. And I wonder what your impression was of her, both in front of the jury and then other times, that the rest of us didn't see.

Judge Perry: There were two sides to Casey. There was the side that was before the jury, where she portrayed the role of a mother who had lost a child, someone who was wrongfully accused, and then you could notice the change and transformation in her when the jury went out. She was very commanding. She took charge of different things and you could see, sometimes, her scolding her attorneys.

Ms. Guthrie: Did you think she was manipulative?

Judge Perry: Very manipulative.

Ms. Guthrie: You almost suggest she was rather two-faced or putting on an act in front of the jury.

Judge Perry: Well, there was always two sides to Casey. There was the public persona that she wanted the jury to see, and there was that side that she showed when the jury was not there.

Ms. Guthrie: And there was a moment when her lawyers came to her to discuss potentially taking a plea deal, pleading to a lesser charge, and she had quite a reaction to that. Can you tell us about it?

Judge Perry: I will never forget that day. One Saturday morning before we were about to begin our session, the lawyers wanted some time to discuss a possible plea to aggravated manslaughter with Casey. They went back in the holding cell and, of course, the waiting area for me was by the holding cell. And all of a sudden you heard shouting coming from the holding cell, some four-letter words coming from the holding cell, and she was quite upset—so upset that one counsel suggested that she was incompetent to proceed.

Ms. Guthrie: Did you think there was sufficient evidence to convict her in this case?

Judge Perry: One of the things that I had to do was to decide whether or not to send this case to a jury. Yes, there was sufficient evidence to sustain a verdict of murder in the first degree in this case.

Ms. Guthrie: What did you think when you opened the envelope and read that verdict?

Judge Perry: Surprise, shock, disbelief.

Ms. Guthrie: I think you told me you read it twice.

Judge Perry: I just wanted to be sure I was reading what I was reading.

Ms. Guthrie: And when you say that, is it because—I don't want to put you on the spot too much, but did you think that the prosecutors had proved her guilt beyond a reasonable doubt?

Judge Perry: Yes, I thought they had proved a—a great case, but you gotta realize this was a circumstantial-evidence case, and all the defense had to do was create that reasonable doubt, and that's what they did.

Ms. Guthrie: You've told me before, you thought this ultimately was a close case on the evidence because of some of the deficiencies in the evidence, and when you have a close case sometimes the lawyering really matters. What did you think of the lawyering in this case?

Judge Perry: Well, the State had better lawyers, but Mr. Baez was very personable and he came across as someone that you would like. It's like somebody trying to sell a used car. Who you gonna buy from? The most likeable salesperson.

Ms. Guthrie: Do you think it was good for the justice system that there were cameras in the court, that this was such a widely followed case?

Judge Perry: Well, in Florida we've always had cameras and I think people need to know how their justice system works, and that's the only way it can work.

Ms. Guthrie: You look at somebody like Casey Anthony, she's out, she's been acquitted, she's free under the law and yet she lives in hiding, she can't really go anywhere, she apparently can't make a living. In your mind, has justice been served to her?

Judge Perry: Well, justice has been served in the sense that the jury has spoken, but justice will finally be served one day by the judge of judges. And she's going to have to deal—live with this and deal with this for the rest of her life.

Ms. Guthrie: Well, Judge Belvin Perry, Jr., it is good to have you in person here, sir. Thank you so much for bringing this pretty unique perspective on the case.

Judge Perry: Thank you.

To say that I was astonished that any judge would do this—*especially* Chief Judge Perry, in the wake of Judge Strickland's expulsion and resignation—would be the understatement of the entire case. Not only is it wildly inappropriate of him professionally to criticize a jury's decision while he is still Chief Judge in that district, it biases the public still further against Casey at a time when there are still actions pending against her—again in his district. Three civil cases, currently on hold because of her bankruptcy proceedings in Federal Bankruptcy Court, are pending against Casey in the Ninth Judicial Circuit, and it is quite arguable that Judge Perry's comments on *The Today Show* have vitiated any chance she still had of a fair trial. Several newspeople in the "Case Against Casey" were in the habit of referring to Judge Perry as the Fourth Prosecutor, and it seems the epithet was a fitting one.

In addition to being delivered in bad faith, the judge's claims were themselves grossly misleading. Judge Perry's chief criticism of Casey as being "manipulative"—as having, as he says, separate faces for the jury and for everyone else—has a simple, completely non-tendentious explanation, with himself at its bottom. Under the very Rules of Decorum that *Judge Perry himself* had posted throughout his courtroom, Casey was *required* to restrain herself while the jury was in the room. When the jury was out, she would frequently take the opportunity to cry more freely, or express frustration, or laugh about the many parts of the trial that seemed so patently absurd as to be humorous—as any human being would.

In order to substantiate this explanation, I here reproduce Judge Perry's Rules of Decorum in full, with the applicable Rule 12 in bold.

IN THE CIRCUIT COURT OF THE NINTH JUDICIAL CIRCUIT, IN AND FOR ORANGE AND OSCEOLA COUNTIES, FLORIDA

ADMINISTRATIVE ORDER NO. 2003-07

ADMINISTRATIVE ORDER ESTABLISHING THE NINTH JUDICIAL CIRCUIT COURTROOM DECORUM POLICY

WHEREAS, in an effort to ensure the effective administration of justice, it is necessary that a policy be established to provide certain basic principles concerning courtroom behavior and decorum in the Ninth Judicial Circuit;

NOW, THEREFORE, I, Belvin Perry, Jr., pursuant to the authority vested in me as Chief Judge of the Ninth Judicial Circuit of Florida under Florida Rule of Judicial Administration 2.050 order that all counsel (including all persons at the counsel table) when appearing in this Court, unless excused by the presiding Judge, shall abide by the following effective immediately:

1. Stand when Court is opened, recessed or adjourned. Stand when addressing, or being addressed by the Court. Stand when the jury enters or retires from the courtroom. When making opening statements, closing arguments or examining witnesses, do not approach either the jury or the witness without the Court's permission. Remain at the lectern unless using exhibits or charts.

2. Address all remarks to the Court, not to opposing counsel or the opposing party.

3. Avoid disparaging personal remarks or acrimony toward opposing counsel and remain wholly detached from any ill feeling between the litigants or witnesses.

4. Refer to all persons, including witnesses, other counsel and the parties by their surnames and not by their first or given names unless the permission of the Court is sought in advance.

5. Only one attorney for each party shall examine, or cross examine each witness. The attorney stating objections, if any, during direct examination, shall be the attorney recognized for cross examination.

6. Counsel should request permission before approaching the bench. Any documents counsel wishes to have the Court examine should be handed to the clerk. Any paper or exhibit not previously marked for identification should first be handed to the clerk to be marked before it is tendered to a witness for his examination; and any exhibit offered in evidence should, at the time of such offer, be handed to opposing counsel.

7. No exhibit, whether marked for identification or not, shall be held in any manner, or placed in any position in the courtroom, that would allow the jury to see the exhibit unless it has been admitted into evidence and permission to publish the exhibit to the jury has been obtained from the Court.

8. In making objections, counsel should state only the legal grounds for the objection and should withhold all further comment or argument unless elaboration is requested by the Court.

9. When examining a witness, counsel shall not repeat or echo the answer given by the witness.

10. Offers of, or request for, a stipulation should be made privately, not within the hearing of the jury.

11. In opening statements and in arguments to the jury, counsel shall not express personal knowledge or opinions concerning any matter in issue.

12. Counsel shall admonish all persons at the counsel table who make gestures, facial expressions, audible comments, or the like, as manifestations of approval or disapproval during the testimony of witnesses, or at any other time. This behavior is strictly prohibited.

13. Counsel shall refrain from attempting to make a re-argument after the Judge has ruled.

14. Counsel shall complete resolution negotiations and advise clients of their settlement options in advance of court hearings.

15. No tobacco use in any form is permitted. No bottles, beverage containers, paper cups or edibles are allowed in the courtroom, except as permitted by the Court. No gum chewing is permitted.

16. Cell phones and pagers should be turned off or in a vibrate mode. Computers should be used with audio off.

DONE AND ORDERED at Orlando, Florida, this 1st day of April, 2003.

/s/ Belvin Perry, Jr.
Belvin Perry, Jr.
Chief Judge

There were a number of other things Judge Perry said during his TV appearance in which he was not quite accurate. One was his claim that "we've always had cameras" in that courtroom. This is simply not true. Cameras were not in that courtroom for the first decade that I was a lawyer there, and it's absolutely up for debate whether they've made, on the whole, a valuable addition since their introduction.

Another, more damning implication was that we had wanted to have time to talk about a possible plea to aggravated manslaughter for Casey, when in fact, this was only our answer to an innuendo from Linda Drane Burdick. Casey, let it be known, *never* had any interest in a negotiated plea. As officers of the court bound by the rules of the Supreme Court, her lawyers were required to explore the possibilities of a plea, no matter how remote; so when Linda had opened that conversation, we talked about it only to the extent of saying that if the State wanted to make a specific offer that would get Casey out of jail, we would discuss it. But when we broached the subject with Casey, her answer was unequivocal: she was not guilty, and she was not going to plead guilty.

It is also extremely disappointing that the judge would admit to overhearing a conversation from the holding cell, when such conversations are required to be absolutely confidential. It may well be that he was in a position to hear such things inadvertently; but in that case he could and should have alerted us to the fact, rather than continuing to listen, and then going on to draw public inferences about what he heard there. Regarding that, furthermore, the fact of the matter is that Casey was indeed very upset when he overheard her—about the suggestion of a guilty plea! And when she rejected it, it was absolutely essential for us to ascertain her competency in order to be sure she was making her decision in conscious free will, and not out of rage engendered by the pressure she had been under for three years.

None of this implies anything characterological about Casey Anthony, or even out-of-the-ordinary as far as defense proceedings go. Yet the average American viewer has little or no experience of such proceedings, or context in which to understand statements about them. The fact that a judge of Belvin Perry's standing would be drawn so strongly to the bright lights as to announce his personal opinion to the world in a manner that may be interpreted as judicial fact, totally contrary to the evidence and insulting to a jury's legitimate verdict, is horrifying.

Yet it may not be so inexplicable, after all. Recently—during the drafting of this manuscript—announcements have surfaced in the press, to the effect that Belvin Perry has been working with television producers to plan a show of his own, *The Judge Perry Show*. How easily one media partnership verges into another in the modern judicial career! Of course, how long this particular one has been in the works, is anyone's guess. But the show is slated to coincide with the judge's planned retirement; in light of which, it seems fair to observe that the duties of one occupation have already begun to supplant those of the other.

EPILOGUE

In the time it took to finalize this manuscript, there has been at least some degree of justice reached in Texas. The judge on trial there, who as a prosecutor had intentionally withheld exculpatory evidence in a homicide case, has been penalized. In exchange for a negotiated plea, he agreed to resign from his judgeship, and permanently lost his license to practice law. He was also sent to jail—if only symbolically and for a very short time. There are many of us around the country who believe this corrupt judge's prison sentence should match that of his victim, the wrongfully imprisoned defendant; yet ironically, it was a defense lawyer who made the deal to keep him out of such a sentence.

For virtually my entire forty-three years as a lawyer, I have seen and heard from colleagues about rampant bias and prejudice in cases just like this one. That said, I will admit, it was a long time before I recognized that there are prosecutors, as there are practitioners of any profession, who are totally devoid of any sense of integrity, dignity or compassion. Yet nowadays the fact is unavoidable. As of this time, the Innocence Project has successfully freed well over three hundred inmates, approximately seventy-five of whom were on death row; while these results cannot all be referred specifically to prosecutorial misconduct or the willful obstruction of justice, many of them can.

More shockingly, in virtually all of the successful Innocence Project cases—three of which I have had the pleasure to assist with in some way—the prosecutors have vigorously opposed DNA testing of old evidence. What reason would a prosecutor or judge, acting in good faith, *ever* have to ignore the possibility of innocence of someone serving time in prison? This is a continuing insult to our basic concepts of justice and objectivity, and further evidence of the kind of obstructive attitude we have discussed throughout this book.

Another form of this obstruction that we encounter with alarming frequency today is the increasing ability of prosecuting attorneys to control the outcome of cases simply by changing or enhancing accusations to suit their whims, rather than being restrained by the evidence to a certain range of accusation. Prosecutors are able to choose what formal charges to allege, and thereby to call different sentencing guidelines into play. These sentencing guidelines, which call for different penalties under different situations, are mathematically affected by such variables as the presence or quantity of narcotics, even in cases not directly related to drug use, or of a firearm, even where there has been no shooting. Manipulating allegations in order to bring these variables into play, a prosecutor can often control the outcome of a trial from the beginning.

Thankfully, there are many federal judges around the country who are increasingly objecting to being bound by these sentencing guidelines; but almost daily the Defense Bar learns of situations in which a judge has been compelled to impose certain mandatory sentences and sanctions because of what prosecutors chose as their accusations. With such mandatory sentences, which in many instances are very severe, even defendants who claim innocence have little choice but to engage in plea bargaining, simply to reduce their risk.

As we strive to become aware of and combat the biases, like these, built into our criminal justice system, we have hardly any need for more from the outside. Events in recent months and years have made it evident that our media organizations, unrestricted by sanctions or control, now stand in a greater position than ever to inflict harm on people's lives and reputations. In light of this, it is far past time for governance to be put in place to prevent the physical assaults and invasions of privacy that these organizations have grown accustomed to demand as their right. They have gone too far; though we need not go too far ourselves in curtailing their behavior, we must not accept the argument that to control them at all is to sacrifice their function in our lives altogether. To call for restraint from our news media is not to suggest that its voice be stifled, but that its accountability be restored—at which point, we will benefit from a renewed appreciation of its value, along with a much-needed improvement of the society it serves.

J. Cheney Mason in 1961 at age 17 on active duty.

On the first day of court.

Casey Anthony with J. Cheney Mason
and Lisabeth Fryer.

Dorothy Clay Sims comforting Casey.

The prosecution team.

Mason and José Baez
discussing court rulings.

J. Cheney Mason and Anthony share
a rare light-hearted moment.

Mason and Baez talking over case details
with prosecutor Linda Drane Burdick.

Mason and Anthony in a moment
of mutual surprise.

Mason expresses exasperation
from a long day at court.

Judge Perry and the attorneys conferring.

Mason, trying to explain what is happening while
also blocking the lip readers.

Discussing the witnesses testimony.

Judge Perry showing interest in the defense table.

Mason at the closing arguments.

Mason at his closing arguments.